Praise for Books on Marriage by Jay Payleitner

52 Things Husbands Need from Their Wives

"As wives, we can choose to be encouragers for our husbands or to be discouragers. Jay Payleitner gives us the inside scoop on what every husband needs. His biblically based perspective and end-of-the-chapter takeaways make this book a practical relationship builder for any couple."

—Karol Ladd
author of *Positive Life Principles for Women*

"Very to the point of what a woman needs to know about her man. After reading these 52 insights, you will better understand that your spouse isn't so weird after all."

—Emilie Barnes
speaker, author, and founder of More Hours in My Day

"Jay is giving away our secrets, and we thank him for it. This is an insightful read, directed to women but educational for all of us, and a practical, user-friendly tool for any wife wanting to better understand the creature she's joined to."

—Joe Dallas
author and speaker

"My husband and I were on the 15-year plan...taking almost 15 years before we began to understand one another. I wouldn't recommend that plan for anyone. Instead, I would wholeheartedly recommend Jay's *52 Things Husbands Need from Their Wives*. Wives—read it, apply it, and begin today to understand the man in your life."

—Kendra Smiley
speaker and author of *Do Your Kids a Favor...Love Your Spouse*

"Jay has done it again. He continues to give us unique insight into building strong family relationships."

—Dan Seaborn
president and founder of Winning at Home, Inc.

"As military families, we spend so much valuable time apart from one another. Knowing how to give my husband what he needs—together or apart—is a treasure. On behalf of all wives, thank you, Jay, for your insight on the one true gift we all can share—love."

—Tara Crooks
cofounder of Army Wife Network and coauthor of
1001 Things to Love About Military Life

"Husbands, step up to being the spiritual leader in your homes. Start by seeking first the kingdom of God and cherishing your wife. Then give your wife a copy of this book. I guarantee you that your marriage will be for the glory of God."

—Harry W. Schaumburg
author of *Undefiled: Redemption from Sexual Sin, Restoration for Broken Relationships*

"This little book is a treasure trove of wisdom and advice for any woman who wants to understand her husband better. Simple (just like your husband) in its approach, it gives an excellent snapshot of what's inside the heart and soul of a man. I highly recommend it!"

—Rick Johnson
author of *Becoming Your Spouse's Better Half*

"Wives, watch out. You are about to be loved, cherished, and surprised!"

—Josh McDowell
author and international speaker

"Don't wince, guys! You're going to love this book! It's biblical, fun, wise, and refreshing, and when your wife 'rises up and calls you blessed,' you'll owe Jay Payleitner for having written it. This is a book every father and husband ought to read, underline, and live."

—Steve Brown
author, seminary professor, and radio teacher on *Key Life*

"Are you taking your wife for granted? That girl you married needs you! And you need her! When a husband and wife seek and find God together, it strengthens families, communities, the church, and the nation. Jay's book is a timely reminder for men that marriage is an awesome gift from God."

—Darrel Billups
executive director of the National Coalition of Ministries to Men

"*52 Things Wives Need from Their Husbands* is a real treasure. It's a realistic and humorous look at married life and how husbands can use their strengths to celebrate and lift up their wives. I wish I'd had this book years ago—it would have saved me a lot of apologizing!"

—Rick Johnson
author of *Becoming Your Spouse's Better Half*

"Just this morning I was asking the Lord to show me how to love my wife better…and then Jay's book *52 Things Wives Need from Their Husbands* arrived in the mail! Now I am all set for the coming year—52 weeks—52 things I can do!"

—Bob Tiede
director of global operations leadership development, Cru

"Jay Payleitner provides men with what we all desperately need—tribal knowledge that gets us more wins and respect from our wives. *52 Things Wives Need from Their Husbands* is brilliant—bite-size intel that packs a massive punch if you follow through. He kills it!"

—Kenny Luck
men's pastor, Saddleback Church
coauthor of the Everyman Bible Studies Series

"Jay Payleitner doesn't talk down to you. You'll be able to relate to the experiences he shares, and laugh and learn along with him. You'll feel empowered and more confident in your marriage. Chances are you'll also like the reaction you get from your wife."

—James Read
executive vice president, Grizzard Communications Group

"I wished I had this book 43 years ago. This book is difficult to put down once you start reading. Jay's humor and straightforwardness have given me many good ideas on how to improve my marriage. I am giving a copy of this book to my son and my son-in-law. I expect them not only to read it but also hand it down to their sons, my grandsons."

—Wayne Sneed
Illinois Fatherhood Initiative

52 WAYS TO CONNECT AS A COUPLE

JAY PAYLEITNER

HARVEST HOUSE PUBLISHERS
EUGENE, OREGON

Cover by Left Coast Design

Cover photo © FCSCAFEINE / Shutterstock

Published in association with the Steve Laube Agency, LLC, 5025 N. Central Ave., #635, Phoenix, Arizona, 85012.

52 WAYS TO CONNECT AS A COUPLE

Copyright © 2016 Jay Payleitner
Published by Harvest House Publishers
Eugene, Oregon 97402
www.harvesthousepublishers.com

ISBN 978-0-7369-6196-7 (pbk.)
ISBN 978-0-7369-6197-4 (eBook)

Library of Congress Cataloging-in-Publication Data
    Names: Payleitner, Jay K.
    Title: 52 ways to connect as a couple / Jay Payleitner.
    Other titles: Fifty-two ways to connect as a couple
    Description: Eugene, Oregon : Harvest House Publishers, 2016. | Includes bibliographical references.
    Identifiers: LCCN 2015038963 | ISBN 9780736961967 (pbk.)
    Subjects: LCSH: Marriage--Religious aspects--Christianity.
    Classification: LCC BV835 .P39 2016 | DDC 248.8/44--dc23 LC record available at http://lccn .loc.gov/2015038963

Printed in the United States of America

15 16 17 18 19 20 21 22 23 24 / BP-KBD / 10 9 8 7 6 5 4 3 2 1

To Alec and Lindsay, Randall and Rachel,
Max and Megan, and Isaac and Kaitlin.
May you discover new ways to love each other more every day.

Contents

Introduction

Whaddaya say? Let's make marriage sexy again. Let's applaud monogamy. Let's give a shout-out for wedded bliss. Let's study our spouses to see how we can serve them and make them deliriously happy.

What if husbands and wives began dating, playing, hanging out, and laughing together? What if couples helped each other chase dreams, feel appreciated, and maybe even break bad habits?

What if—miraculously—you and your beloved never slammed another door in anger and completely stopped arguing about dirty dishes, in-laws, and credit card bills?

Husbands: What if you muted the playoff game and actually turned to make eye contact when your wife asks a question?

Wives: What if you stopped trashing your husband when you talk with your girlfriends?

Do you kiss in the kitchen? Do you put sex on the calendar? Do you pray together? Are you saving up for a second honeymoon? If not, why not start now?

Here are some ideas you can use this very week to connect as a couple. Pack a picnic. Buy new bed linens. Go to a drive-in movie. Leave a love note. Rent a Porsche. Rent a tandem. Or maybe visit his or her old neighborhood.

Here's an even better idea. Let's start a campaign to build lasting monuments to men and women who have stayed married for 40, 50, 60 years. Oh, wait—those monuments already exist! They're called families. With kids, grandkids, and great-grandkids. A loving family is way better than any statue or shrine.

Guys and gals, this book is about your marriage and how you can be more intentional about connecting as a couple. There is no risk, no downside. And the benefits are many. For you, your family, your community, and the world.

For some reason, marriage and monogamy have been getting a bad rap in recent years. Don't believe it. God designed marriage to bring joy, purpose, fulfillment, satisfaction, and even spiritual closeness to a man and woman in a lifelong commitment. In the original blueprint, marriage was a blessing. God didn't create marriage to be a burden or a grind. Why would he do that?

No doubt, authentic intimacy takes work, dedication, communication, honesty, forgiveness, and sensitivity. But the rewards far outweigh any effort. The two-sided commitment is what makes it fun. A husband and wife should expect to invest a lifetime figuring out what makes each other tick. And how to tickle each other.

Your assignment today is to convince your husband or wife to read this book *with* you. Maybe even reading it together out loud. It's quite doable. Painless. Even amusing.

The chapters are short. Nothing here will make you feel guilty, weak, or worthless. Actually, most chapters will leave you empowered and optimistic.

Okay? Ready? Commit to sampling the first few chapters and see how it goes. I'm pretty sure you'll make it through the entire book. Along the way you will surely uncover some new insights into how you can love your spouse the way they deserve to be loved. And you can expect the same.

"One of the nicest things to be in the whole wide world is half of a couple."

—Jay Payleitner

1

Couples Need...

To Elevate Expectations

This book will not save your marriage. This book will not tangle or untangle your bedsheets. This book will not cause you to laugh and love and live in peaceful harmony all the days of your lives. Only you can make those things happen.

How? Most importantly, raise your expectations. You can't really expect to connect as a couple until you embrace the full promise and potential of marriage. Your connection with your spouse is the most valuable and rewarding relationship you have on earth. More than with your parents, your kids, your best friend, or your business partner.

To get the most out of this book and the most out of life, recognize that your marriage relationship is intimately intertwined with every aspect of your existence. Your spouse was given to you (and vice versa) as a helpmate, partner, advisor, encourager, and sounding board as your life journey unfolds. Time spent with your husband or wife should become a sanctuary in which you can refocus your goals and reinvigorate your resolve to fight the good fight.

That doesn't mean married life is some kind of fairy-tale existence. On occasion, there will be a short circuit in communications. Some poor choices will be made. Maybe he reinvents himself for a season, and you don't like the new version so much. Maybe she's expressed some desires or demands that are not top priorities for you. Maybe you feel as if you're in a rut, on the edge of a cliff, or at the bottom of a deep, dry well. No matter what, don't buy the lie—marriage is not the problem. In fact, *it may very well be the solution.*

Consider the big picture for a moment. Marriage is the perfect design for life on this planet. It permanently connects two individuals with different gifts, abilities, desires, and body parts. They fit together quite nicely. Two become one, which means they challenge, support, and comfort each other. Because of the marriage partnership, the lives of two flawed souls are continually upgraded, repaired, and enhanced.

You remember saying these words: "To have and to hold from this day forward, for better, for worse, for richer, for poorer, in sickness or in health, to love and to cherish till death do us part."

At the time—and to most people—that meant you were promising to hang tough in good times and bad. But consider this: Might it be possible the marriage vows are part of a celestial promise that the two of you are now perfectly equipped to handle anything that comes your way? Think of it this way. From this day forward—if you have and hold each other—you can expect to find meaning and joy even if you happen to be poor or sick. By loving and cherishing till death, anything that seems to be happening for worse will have time to turn for better. It's all right there in your vows.

The marriage relationship must have great significance and power. The crowning achievement of God's creation was a man and woman coming together for the first time in history.

> So God created mankind in his own image,
>   in the image of God he created them;
>   male and female he created them.
>
> God blessed them and said to them, "Be fruitful and
> increase in number; fill the earth and subdue it"...
> God saw all that he had made, and it was very good.
> And there was evening, and there was morning—the sixth
> day (Genesis 1:27,31).

On God's first recorded seven-day workweek, he created everything that exists outside of heaven—light, sky, water, land, stars, planets, plants, and animals. The very last thing he did was make man and woman in his image, instructing *both of them* to be fruitful, multiply, and subdue the earth. Only then did God rest.

It appears God has some high expectations for your marriage. Do you?

After your honeymoon, did you set your marriage on cruise control and settle into some unfulfilling routine? Or are you following God's plan to work together to "subdue" the earth? That's the goal, and you need to put your heads together to figure out what that means for you and your beloved. It will require you to look beyond your individual selfish needs. It means you need to see your spouse as a partner created by God. To reach your full potential, you need to see the beauty, blessing, and value in your marriage relationship.

Marriage is not just a social construct that happens to be a convenient arrangement for paying a mortgage, sharing household chores, having an available sex partner, or raising kids. Your marriage can, should, and will be awesome. Expect it.

— Question to Ask Out Loud —

What part of the earth do we want to subdue together?

"Marriage is an adventure, like going to war."

—G.K. CHESTERTON

2

Couples Need…

To Stop Guessing

Don't answer this out loud.

Wives, would you rather have your husband surprise you with a small bouquet of flowers or a small box of chocolates? Decide now.

Husbands, would your bride rather have you surprise her with a small bouquet of flowers or a small box of chocolates? Decide now.

Now compare your answers.

When I ask those questions of an audience of married couples, the answers match about 60 percent of the time. Not bad, right? Except that means four out of ten well-intentioned guys are bringing home the wrong surprise.

Of course, any smart wife expresses delight with any gift at any time. If she doesn't, then that's a completely different set of problems. Also, in an auditorium filled with husbands and wives, there are most certainly guys who pretty much never bring home any surprises at all. Which is yet another kind of problem.

Also worth noting, some wives will sincerely say, "Either is wonderful. It truly is the thought that counts." While a statistically insignificant amount of women care for neither flowers nor chocolate.

All that to say, you may not know each other as well as you think you do. Is that a problem? Not at all. One of the joys of marriage is discovering new things about your spouse, which should continue to happen even decades into your marriage. Just a month ago, I learned that Rita spent an enjoyable summer of her youth as an intern at an art studio in Chicago. That fresh insight led to all kinds of new memory sharing and discoveries about the girl I thought I knew. (And now that I think about it, I don't know how Rita would answer the flowers versus chocolate question.)

The idea that mysteries remain even after years of marriage lends itself to another reason to stick around and see how life unfolds. Some of those mysteries will reveal themselves naturally over time. Some are worth a bit of intentional probing so the two of you can live in harmony and uncover fresh opportunities to bring each other delight, pleasure, and satisfaction.

Let's consider a few more questions beyond flowers and chocolates. There are no wrong or right answers—there is only insight to be gained into your spouse's minor preferences and deep desires. The strategy to make this little exercise work is for you each to come up with your own answers and then compare notes.

Vacation. Beach, mountaintop, or big city?

Retirement. Florida, Arizona, near the grandkids, or "I like it right here"?

Massage. Foot rub or full body?

Evening at home. TV, movie rental, game night, or curling up with a good book?

$6,000 bonus windfall. Pay bills, invest, vacation splurge, or buy something for the home?

Christmas tree. Fake or fir?

Skiing. Snow or water?

Instant communication. Call or text?

$100 tickets. Symphony, Broadway show, playoff game, or rock and roll?

End-of-year gift. Local charity, missionary friend, orphan sponsorship, or trusted ministry?

Christmas tradition. Open one gift at a time or everyone rips in at once?

Breakfast. In bed, a local bistro, or at the kitchen table with the newspaper?

You get the idea, right? Considering this list, it occurs to me that these would be excellent questions to ask each other *before* you get married. Even though there are no real wrong answers here, these preferences are well worth knowing. It might be slightly earth-shattering to learn that you've been going to the beach every winter for the last ten years and your spouse would have rather been at a downtown Hilton. Or that you've been chopping down a live tree every Christmas when a plastic tree with zero needles in the carpet would have suited you both just fine. Or maybe you always stopped at the foot rub, but now you know you can explore other regions as well.

You can play the "Would you rather...?" game anytime or anyplace. I recommend it. If you learn something particularly surprising, let me know. But don't play too long or dig too deep. It's always nice to save some mystery for another day.

— Question to Ask Out Loud —

Next month we're going to _____. Would you rather fly, drive, or take the train? Should we go alone or with another couple? Would you rather stay overnight or drive home in the dark? Would you rather not go at all?

> *"What counts in making a happy marriage is not so much how compatible you are, but how you deal with incompatibility."*
> —George Levinger

3

Couples Need…

To Work on Your Marriage Together

This is a book for both husbands and wives. But unofficial statistics I just made up indicate that 92.3 percent of the time it's the wife who buys a book like this. Her hope and dream is for the two of them to read the book together. For most couples, that just ain't gonna happen.

Before going any further, let's take a moment right here in chapter 3 to congratulate that small percentage of couples who are digging into this together. Or it might be time for you—the wonderful, thoughtful, beautiful, hopeful wife—to throw this book at your husband's head and say, "Hey, let's do this together. It'll be fun!"

If that doesn't feel like the right option, just keep reading and make sure your husband gets a verbal summary of the main points. Careful however. When wives read relationship books, get marriage advice from friends, or go to counseling alone, there's a tendency to see only one side of the argument.

Often, the wife's summary is really just an excuse to bash her husband. She will carefully extract critical passages that prove some point she has been making for years.

"See! You're *not* supposed to leave boot prints on the linoleum."

"See! You're *not* supposed to side with your mom all the time."

"See! You're *not* supposed to take me to a sports bar for dinner and spend the entire meal looking over my shoulder at some televised game you don't even care about."

Giving wives ammunition to snipe at their husbands is not my intention at all. If you happen to find yourself using this book as a battering ram to crush the spirit of your devoted husband, please slip it quietly onto your bookshelf and back away before someone (or some marriage) gets hurt.

Yes, there are moments in this book that instruct a husband to wipe his feet, cut the apron strings, and make reservations at a TV-free restaurant. (There are also moments in this book that give specific instructions to wives.) But most of these 52 chapters focus on *positive* strategies for connecting as a couple, including conversations to have, memories to remember, places to visit, and reasons to celebrate God's gift of marriage.

With that in mind, I totally encourage you—on 52 separate occasions—to take turns reading these chapters to each other right out loud. You can read some of them in four minutes. None of them will take longer than ten. What might take a few extra minutes is the single question at the end of each chapter.

So, ladies, no nagging, no silent treatment, no withholding sex, and no book throwing. Tell him you love him and want to stay blissfully married forever and ever. Then simply ask him to give it a try.

For those guys who are already reading this book out loud with your brides, your reward: three extra kisses.

— Question to Ask Out Loud —

Should we try reading this book together every night? Over breakfast? Or should we not stress about maintaining a firm schedule, and just keep moving the bookmark one chapter at a time when we find a few minutes during the week?

"The great happiness in life is the conviction that we are loved—loved for ourselves, or rather, loved in spite of ourselves."

—Victor Hugo

4

Couples Need...

To See the Seasons

What season of life are you in? Each one brings its own blessings. The irony is that in most seasons, you're too busy to appreciate it at the time.

Engaged and filled with hope. Newlyweds discovering each other. Young marrieds thinking you have all the answers. New parents wondering and worrying about the future. Seasons when you are broke, then wealthy, then broke again. Times of extended illness or crises. Caretaker for your parents or in-laws. The season of blurred activities, balancing work and family. Watching teenagers turn into adults. Watching young adult children from a distance. Listening to the echoes of an empty nest. Welcoming boomerang kids back home. Grandparenting. Caring for each other in gratitude and love.

Seasons come with their own set of joys, challenges, and expectations. Seasons overlap. Seasons come to an end and then come back again. You can ease in and out of seasons. Or they begin and end abruptly. Some are filled with hope. Some are filled with despair.

Seasons can bring the two of you closer. Or drive a wedge.

My favorite season was when the five kids were all still at home and Alec was beginning his college search while Rae Anne was getting ready for kindergarten. Randy, Max, and Isaac were active in school and sports, and there were at least 15 kid-related events on the calendar every week. At the time, I didn't realize the preciousness of each moment. I probably lost my cool once in a while because of tight schedules, messy rooms, late carpools, lost sports gear, and unexpected escalating expenses. I have a handful of regrets, but I made things right whenever I could.

During your next season of life, you may discover something about your beloved that surprises the heck out of you.

For almost 30 years, Rita was a behind-the-scenes kind of gal. Working hard in volunteer positions at church and our local schools, taking no credit, always being a humble servant. Six years ago, a neighbor who was stepping down from the Saint Charles City Council encouraged Rita to run for office. She did. And she won. Suddenly, my modest bride is expanding her comfort zone and taking a firm stand on zoning laws, being interviewed by the media, and officiating at ribbon cuttings and other public ceremonies.

All of which leaves me a little torn. I'm wonderfully proud of Rita. I know her efforts on behalf of our city have been worth every meeting and her many hours studying the issues. She has become a thoughtful, conservative voice for fiscal responsibility and standing firm on moral issues. But sometimes I also feel a little out of the loop. That may sound selfish, but it's an honest assessment.

On the other hand, the pluses definitely outweigh any negatives. Right when we thought we'd be empty nesters, wondering what to do with ourselves, her responsibilities have led to a wide range of new experiences. Not just for Rita, but for me as well. I'll escort her on city business as she surveys a piece of property or dedicates a new construction project. Sometimes I'll even throw on a sport coat to be "arm candy" at a fund-raiser, art show, or grand opening. I haven't missed a parade yet, waving and whistling at the city council float.

This has been a totally unexpected season in our lives. Nationally, I'm a bestselling author. Locally, I'm the alderman's husband. Neither of those titles were on anyone's radar screen when we walked down the aisle.

The lesson here is this. Wives and husbands, I urge you to make the most of every season in your married life. Each one comes with its own joys and frustrations, responsibilities and surprises, blessings and sorrows, beginnings and ends.

Ladies, if the honeymoon is barely over and you're wondering what happened to that handsome, attentive, and generous fiancé, give him time. Gentlemen, I know you're wondering a few things too.

If you're up to your armpits in baby drool, soccer schedules, broken appliances, and bad hair days, please remember this exhausting season doesn't last forever. You'll miss it more than you could ever imagine. (Take lots of photos.)

Maybe you're courageously enduring a season of true agony. You have a teenager heading the wrong direction. Illness or loss has brutalized your family. Maybe you can't even identify the problem, but a dark cloud has settled over your home. You may need some professional help to guide you into a brighter season, and that's okay too. Every spring begins in winter.

The goal, of course, is to reach the season of appreciation and reflection. That's when you get a chance to look back and make sense out of the ups and downs of all the other seasons. The longer you walk with God, the more you get small glimpses of heaven and how all things work toward God's ultimate purpose for your life.

That final season is when you'll fully realize that your beloved was a gift from God, who knew exactly what you needed and found your perfect match.

> Live happily with the woman you love through all the meaningless days of life that God has given you under the sun. The wife God gives you is your reward for all your earthly toil (Ecclesiastes 9:9 NLT).

Wrapping up this idea: The secret to living happily through the seasons is to understand that her needs will change and his needs will change. Husbands and wives can actually bring meaning to life when they look at each season as a chance to rediscover each other. To celebrate and console. To give and receive. To carry each other. To serve. And be served.

Navigating through all those tumultuous seasons of life will lead a husband and wife to a depth of love and respect that mere newlyweds could not possibly understand.

— Question to Ask Out Loud —

What highs and lows are we experiencing in this season? What will you miss when we enter the next season?

"Grow old along with me!
The best is yet to be,
The last of life, for which the first was made."

—Robert Browning, *Rabbi Ben Ezra*

5

Couples Need...

To List Likes

Here's a strategy I've been endorsing for years: Literally make a list of things your spouse likes. Not huge, extravagant, budget-breaking trips or gifts. Small things. Things you can share with each other on a weekly or daily basis.

The very act of creating such a list works on about five different levels. You spend intentional time recalling positive experiences with each other. As you remember those experiences, you imagine a future in which you can relive those moments. You begin to realize that you are the only person in this world who can make such a list and the one person in the world who can truly fulfill the needs of your beloved. You experience the joy of meeting those needs. You experience the reciprocal joy of having your needs met. (More on that later.)

If this is not making sense—or if the value of these lists feels a little unverifiable—maybe that's because you haven't made your list yet. As a public service, allow me to present a list of things *I* like. And if my bride, Rita, happens to see it...well, then good for me! She is already well aware of many of these items and ideas, but it never hurts to remind her.

Here are some things I like: down pillows, sock monkeys, petting doggies, warm feet, a good chopped salad, grilled pork chops, strawberry-rhubarb pie, bookstores, boxers, brick sidewalks, holding hands with my wife, stopping on the stairs with her one step above for a kiss, comfy jeans, campfires, well-formed quotations, meaningful song lyrics, "The Star Spangled Banner," watching my kids compete, beef jerky, black Sharpies, bending paper clips, a good pair of scissors, finding a piece of Scripture that applies to a real-life challenge, lying in the grass on a sunny day, strolling through a flea market or art fair with my wife, son, and daughter-in-law, and so on.

Some of these items might take a bit of an effort. But none are insurmountable or burdensome. Most are cheap. Many are free. All will put a smile on my face, and that's a goal my wife usually sees as worthwhile.

For the sake of fairness, here's a list of things Rita likes: fireworks, parades, a powder room for company that says welcome, babies, cute babies, gurgly babies, pretty much all babies, television commercials with babies, scones, frozen Cokes, sparkly glassware on her Thanksgiving dinner table, hanging out with her children, bling for Christmas, warm feet, clean kitchen counters, old sitcoms, sitting in the sun with a book, fresh flowers, fresh snow, drinking straws, craft magazines, and so on.

So now are you tracking? This book will not be filled with a bunch of long homework assignments that never get finished. Each chapter ends with a mere one or two questions to ask out loud and get you talking. Nothing burdensome, I promise. But I'm going to insist the two of you stop right now and make those two lists.

It's not optional. Grab a couple yellow pads or open a couple Word docs. He makes a list of what she likes. She makes a list of what he likes. Take ten minutes. Or take three days. To get you started, you have my complete permission to steal any relevant items from Rita's and my lists. Go for it. I'll wait.

Done already? Super. Then begin today delighting your spouse with the listed items and ideas. Feel free to exchange lists and sift through memories and emotions connected to each entry. For instance, my appreciation of sock monkeys can be traced back to one particular silly shopping trip with my kids. Singing the national anthem sparks memories of softball games when our daughter played at West Point. Rita's fondness for parades is especially amusing because as alderman, she represents the city of Saint Charles in several annual holiday parades down Main Street.

The point is that you know more about your spouse than does anyone else in the world. Which means you are the best person in the world to fill their needs and desires. Which makes marriage different from any other relationship in the world. That's all part of God's plan.

Moving forward, give each other permission to add and subtract items without judgment. These ever-changing lists can provide a chance to learn new things about each other. If your spouse adds an item or two, look at them as opportunities to delight, not demands to be met.

Which brings us to a few words of warning. Please don't use these lists as some kind of inventory of obligations. When your husband or wife fulfills one of these desires, the last thing you want to do is gripe, "It's about time. How long has that been on my list?" That attitude takes all the joy out of giving *and* receiving.

Also, you did not just create two lists of bargaining chips. Some wives might be thinking, *I can use this list to con him, distract him, or bribe him into giving me some of the things I want.* Some husbands might be thinking, *If I do what she likes, she'll do what I like.* That's a popular game for married couples, but it's no way to run a marriage. Marriage (and these lists) should focus on the idea of two becoming one. A verse that appears in the Bible three times—Genesis chapter 2, Matthew chapter 19, and Ephesians chapter 5—reminds us that a man leaves his father and mother and is united to his wife, and they become one flesh.

United as one flesh. Your hearts, needs, and desires are inseparable. In other words, *if you give your spouse what he or she likes, it will give you joy as well.*

Finally, these lists are probably best kept private between you and your beloved. As a matter of fact, I kept a few things off the above lists because they are simply none of your business.

— Question to Ask Out Loud —

When can we exchange lists?

"The one thing we can never get enough of is love.
And the one thing we never give enough of is love."

—Henry Miller

6

Couples Need…

To Haunt the Old Haunts

My wife was in a street gang on the southwest side of Chicago near Midway Airport. The Clicky Chicks didn't terrorize the neighborhood, but they stuck together, giving each other the unique kind of confidence eighth-grade girls need to grow up in the city.

On hot summer days, the girls would either walk around the air-conditioned Midway terminal, take the Archer Express to Oak Street Beach, or go to the home of the one Clicky Chick who had an above-ground pool. At one time, privately owned pools were not legal in Chicago unless you were a cop, fireman, or teacher. That was one of the concessions to the unions because first responders and teachers were required to live in the city limits. Only in Chicago would that kind of deal be made.

Once a week, Rita's little brother would sit on the fence and wait for the trash collectors to come down the alley. On one occasion, Kevin showed up at school with a pocketful of Kennedy half dollars. He told the nuns he "found them in the prairie" on his way to school. That's what city kids called any vacant lot filled with weeds. As was the routine, Rita had to come down to Sister Anne Marie's office to clear up Kevin's tall tales. The half dollars were actually an innocent birthday gift.

The reason I know these stories is because I've driven past the cop's house, walked down the alley, seen the 40- by 80-foot "prairie," and peeked in the window of Saint Mary Star of the Sea School. I've even bought soda bread and corned beef from Winston's Deli, where the Clicky Chicks would stop for Irish sweets and treats.

As a high school freshman, Rita moved reluctantly out to the far west suburbs, which worked out well for me. If you married your high school sweetheart, you might think you know everything about them. But I promise you don't. If you met after high school, there are even more mysteries to be uncovered. You can pull out old yearbooks and ask random questions—which would lead to an amusing evening. But it takes an intentional trip to the old neighborhood for the memories to really begin tumbling back.

So make that happen. Drive slow and let your husband or wife whisper memories, point, and smile. That street corner. That window. That now-empty storefront.

For some, stirring up the past uncovers swirls of memories that might have an edge of remorse or grief. If that's true for your beloved, this journey back home may come with an unexpected dividend. Taking a devoted spouse on a nostalgia tour may be a gift of sweet release. Your life together, which now includes a solid marriage built on love and trust, can sweep away a dusty gathering of regrets. *Hey, it turned out okay. I turned out okay. Look how far I've come.*

It might take a Sunday afternoon drive or a cross-country expedition. You could do it with or without the kids. It might be part of spending the holiday with the in-laws. Consider scheduling your trip around a high school reunion or see if that old street gang wants to get together for one more rumble.

Make sure you carve out enough time to hold a conversation with one or two old-timers who remember the not-so-distant past. Don't leave the neighborhood until you can picture your spouse at nine years old looking at stars out a bedroom window, jumping rope in the driveway, selling lemonade on the corner, or climbing monkey bars in the schoolyard.

Let your beloved do most of the talking that day. And then schedule another jaunt to your old neighborhood so the two of you can retrace your old footsteps.

— Question to Ask Out Loud —

Who's living in the house where you grew up? And where did you cool off on hot summer days?

_____

"Memories are the key not to the past, but to the future."

—CORRIE TEN BOOM

_____

Couples Need...

To Kiss in the Kitchen for the Sake of the Kids

As the nursery rhyme goes more or less, "First comes love, then comes marriage, then comes a kid—or two or three or four—in a baby carriage."

Your marriage may or may not include offspring, now or in the future. But no matter what, you need to know that modeling a healthy marriage relationship has a positive impact on the next generation and beyond.

If you are a mom and dad, your immediate circle of influence is obvious. You have the clear-cut privilege of creating a launchpad for your children and their children. Members of the [your last name here] family are counting on you to establish a nurturing environment and legacy of love and commitment.

Recent studies reveal that children of divorce have a rougher time in life. The following stats are tendencies, not absolutes, so let's keep our hopes high for young people in general. But the research is valid.

- Children of divorce are roughly twice as likely to see their own marriage end in divorce.[1]

- Children of divorced parents are roughly twice as likely to drop out of high school.[2]

- Children of divorce are at a greater risk to experience injury, asthma, headaches, and speech defects.[3]

- Teenagers in single-parent families and in blended families are three times more likely to need psychological help.[4]

- Seventy percent of long-term prison inmates grew up in broken homes.[5]

Flipping those numbers upside down, it seems evident that while unstable marriages drag kids down, mothers and fathers committed to each other for the long haul are improving their children's chances for a secure and happy life. That idea shouldn't cause panic or pressure. It's really just a statistical reminder that your marriage matters to your kids.

So kudos to you. And congratulations on being committed to your spouse. Just by picking up this book, you're expressing a desire to build something significant that lasts beyond your own earthly tenure.

Take this opportunity to go a step further. Tell your kids stories about your courtship and romance. Let them know your wedding day was a blessing and your marriage is solid as a rock. Kiss in the kitchen. Do a weekend away once in a while. Secure a lock on your bedroom door. You don't have to tell your kids what goes on behind that door. As they get older, they'll figure it out. Teenagers don't want to think about such things, but they'll know. And they'll be glad.

— Question to Ask Out Loud —

Do our kids know we love, cherish, and crave each other?

---

*"Blessed are those who fear the L*ORD*,*
who find great delight in his commands.
Their children will be mighty in the land;
the generation of the upright will be blessed.
Wealth and riches are in their houses,
and their righteousness endures forever."

—PSALM 112:1-3

Couples Need...

To Put Sex on the Calendar

Please do not write the word "SEX" or "YOWZA" on the calendar that hangs on your fridge. It's in bad taste. And it will surely frighten guests and family members. Also, do not put exclamation points or asterisks on your digital Outlook Web App that links to your entire office. It will only raise questions you don't want to answer.

But do—on occasion—schedule sex a few days in advance. You don't have to literally write it down, but the goal is for you and your beloved to confirm your mutual intentions clearly. Then each in your own way can invest the hours beforehand preparing your heart, mind, soul, body, and bedroom for the event.

While impromptu romance adds an air of excitement to a relationship, premeditated sex has a wide range of benefits that you won't appreciate until you've tried it.

Anticipation. Much of the pleasure of a vacation, outing, or party comes from the promise of what's to come. If a husband knows for sure that he's going to make love with his bride on Friday night, the last few days of his work week are quite literally more pleasant. He can lose a business deal or get yelled at by the boss, but it's okay. He still knows Friday is going to end well.

Appreciation. If both of you are looking forward to the promise of the evening, there's a good chance you'll be a little nicer to each other the day or two in advance. It may be truer for the guy, but he's going to be extra careful to not blow his chance. He may even show his appreciation with a little bonus attention, an offer to do an extra chore around the house, or a token of affection in the form of flowers, chocolate, and so on. It's not a transaction, but there is a sense of gratitude and devotion that comes with the prospect of your time together.

Creativity. A confirmed date on the calendar leads to confidence. Confidence leads to the freedom to be a bit more creative in the bedroom. There will be no specific examples here. But there's no doubt that 48 hours of anticipation allows time for the imagination to conjure up all kinds of options. You've been warned.

Preparation. A nice meal. Fresh linens. New lingerie. A relaxing bath. Setting the scene with candles, music, and so on. It wouldn't hurt to pick up the dirty socks and clear the empty microwave popcorn bag from the end table either. For sure, there are more things that can break the mood than can establish the mood. So take care to do whatever you need to do to keep a good thing going. That may even include trimming your toenails.

Follow through. Don't take scheduled sex lightly. If you both clearly agreed to it, there's a 97 percent chance your spouse has been doing the anticipation, appreciation, creative musings, and preparation outlined above. There would need to be a pretty good reason for breaking your date.

On the other hand, dedicated and devoted husbands and wives like you understand that plans carved in stone sometimes get broken. You will want to minimize stress that afternoon so the migraine doesn't kick in. You will want to eat light so tummy troubles don't erupt. You will want to make sure kids and pets are safe and secure so interruptions are minimized.

But things do happen. Sump pumps fail. Kids have bad dreams. Bedbugs could invade your pillowcases. Raccoons could set up housekeeping in your attic. TV bulletins could deliver news of an escaped convict in your neighborhood. A traveling circus could mistakenly start pitching their tents in your side yard just as you're getting ready for bed. It's quite likely that he will express a desire to stay the course. But it's also quite likely that she will want to take a rain check.

Gentlemen, cuddle up next to her and let her know it's perfectly okay. And set another date for tomorrow night. Or the next. Or the next.

You can wait, right? After all, we're not animals.

— Question to Ask Out Loud —

How about Friday night?

"Be completely humble and gentle;
be patient, bearing with one another in love."

—Ephesians 4:2

9

Couples Need…

To Stop Having Pretend Conversations

A couple exactly your age is sitting at a table in a kitchen that looks a lot like your kitchen. She's talking. He's listening. Except that really he's not.

In many ways, he looks as if he's listening. He actually was for a while. The topic of the conversation wasn't particularly interesting to him. But he loves his wife and sincerely cares about everything she cares about simply because she cares about it. For several minutes, he was even nodding in agreement and adding a thoughtful verbal response every now and then. And then his mind went somewhere else.

Maybe something she said triggered thoughts of an old girlfriend. Maybe he glanced at a headline in the sports page that mentioned a player on his fantasy football team. Maybe his stomach reminded him that he hadn't eaten in 90 minutes. Maybe he had heard this story before and was trying to remember how it will end, but his mind rabbit-trailed off to three other stories.

Have you been there? As a couple, have you had any pretend conversations? How many? And how long did they go?

Please know it's a universal problem. While it is pretty much the guy's fault 97 percent of the time, don't anyone start pointing fingers and letting it ruin your day. Wives, you may be not-so-amused to know that it happens a lot more than you think. Often, husbands get away with it. Their brilliant maneuvers and tap dancing are really quite astonishing feats.

How does such a conversation unfold? For a while, the loving husband is actively engaged, asking questions and giving input. But before long, the wife finds herself talking without interruption for several minutes. His side of the conversation has diminished to an occasional nod and affirmative grunt. Then she wraps up with some kind of verbal proposal that requires a response. Something like, "Can you do that?" or "How does next Thursday sound?" or "That's my suggestion—what do you think?"

Once he realizes that a question has been asked, instant panic ensues. Because he's had plenty of practice, his emotions are imperceptible to her. But believe me, he is internally frantic.

His mushy, unfocused mind becomes keenly aware of any visual clues pertaining to what she might have been talking about. *Is she holding theatre tickets? An IRS bulletin? A brochure from a cruise line? An email from the high school dean? A sales flyer from Old Navy?* Then he searches his recent memory banks to see if somehow he can recall a train of thought from before his mind wandered. He strains his brain to catch a few stray words still lingering in his ear canals but not yet deleted. Then he takes the ultimate gamble. He responds with actual words. He doesn't say yes or no because that would be committing to something to which he may not want to commit. He also doesn't say, "Let me think about it," because he knows his bride might say, "What is there to think about?" and then his goose is really cooked.

So that's when he begins the verbal tap dance. This Oscar-worthy performance consists of hesitantly delivering short, nonspecific, unfinished statements that he hopes will lead his wife to add more information until the original question becomes clear. Things like "Well…" "I…uh…" "That would…" Done properly, it looks as if he is actually pondering the question and all its implications. Before long, there's a good chance she will continue the discussion and he will gain just enough clues to catch up and catch on. The tap dance strategy is a true art form and not for the squeamish or faint of heart. But husbands, be warned. If your wife knows you're tap dancing, you're in for a real tough day.

Which brings us to the best strategy for any couple who finds themselves in the middle of a standoff at the kitchen table. First, acknowledge that it's going to happen. Second, recognize that there's no evil intent here. It's just a harmless scenario that can happen anytime after the honeymoon for even the most committed couples.

So how should you respond? If she's smart, she needs to expect it and accept it. Because when the dust settles, she's very likely going to get her way.

If he's smart, he needs to confess, apologize, and beg her to clarify her question one more time. And then—because he's been given a reprieve—he needs to give her the answer she wants to hear. "Yes, I can do that." "Thursday is fine." "I think your suggestion is brilliant."

After a few years of marriage, you'll both be fairly adept at recognizing the topics that don't hold his interest and situations in which his mind is prone to wander. After thousands of conversations, a good-humored wife will call his bluff even before he begins his pretend conversation. She knows the signs and will say with a smile, "You're not listening, are you?" As frightening as those words sound, they are really a blessing. A quick confession and short apology will move the conversation to where it should already be going. He should respond with something like, "Sorry, I was distracted for a moment. What was that last thing you said?" A smart wife won't berate her husband because she knows she has the upper hand. She will simply restate the question and include obvious hints that guide the husband toward the answer she wants to hear.

In summary, when a spouse's mind wanders, the result should not be World War III and a week of nuclear winter. Instead, consider it a fresh opportunity to celebrate your commitment to one another.

Shorter stories from her and a little more focus from him wouldn't hurt either.[6]

— Question to Ask Out Loud —

What is one strategy or signal we could use to let each other know that a particular conversation is not just chitchat, but carries some real importance?

"When a woman is talking to you,
listen to what she says with her eyes."

—Victor Hugo

10

Couples Need…

To Do Stuff

Pretend for a moment that you're the handsome couple riding bikes on the cover of this book. Where are you? How far will you be riding? What are you laughing about? How will the rest of the day unfold? And how about your evening?

It's nice to think about such things. It's also pretty clear that doing activities together helps you connect as a couple. Any endeavor. Any age. Any measure of success.

You don't have to climb down into the Grand Canyon and camp overnight. Maybe just standing side by side and enjoying the view is enough. You don't have to become members of the World DanceSport Federation, but taking a six-week ballroom dancing course through your park district could be just the ticket. You don't have to win the Mid-American Canoe and Kayak Race down the Fox River that begins in my hometown every June. But paddling down a gently flowing waterway and maybe "accidentally" overturning your canoe would be just as fun. Or maybe even more fun.

So, what stuff might you do? Let's start with the obvious and go from there.

Rent bikes, a tandem bike, a canoe, or kayaks. You'll burn some energy and probably discover some neighborhoods or river bends you've never seen before. Make sure you schedule some recovery (and cuddle) time afterword.

Rollerblades or ice skates. Don't invest in skates unless you do this several times a year. Even midsize towns have shops or park district huts where you can rent footgear for use in designated rinks and paths. Race each other. Hold hands. Show off your double salchow. And get ready to pick each other up after bruising your tailbones.

Segway tour. Quite a few cities offer a chance to jump on your very own two-wheeled, gyroscope-balanced vehicle and follow a tour guide through their bustling streets. You'll see sculptures, fountains, bridges, and other landmarks. But the best part is how remarkably easy Segways are to navigate.

Canyon hiking, rock climbing, snorkeling, hang gliding, white-water rafting, cross-country skiing, zip lining, or bungee jumping. Mostly for younger couples, but how old do you really feel?

Hot air balloon rides, horseback riding, Jeep tours, or renting a convertible for the weekend. Some adventures don't require you to be in peak physical shape. Although fear of heights, equine allergies, queasy tummies, and windblown hair may be worth considering.

Disc golf. I can't recommend golf for couples. If you're both pretty good, then go for it. But for most couples, one laborious round of golf is a recipe for relational disaster. However, spending an hour or so at one of the many disc golf courses sprouting up around the country might be a delightful bonding experience as you learn the strategies and techniques together. You can call it exercise, but it's more like a walk in the park with a dose of competition.

And then don't be afraid to scoff at traditional gender roles and suggest some activities that will instantly get the attention of your spouse:

Salsa dancing, ballroom dancing, or square dancing. If a husband suggests this for his wife, I promise she will look at him sideways and say, "Really?" It will be an evening you'll always remember. Maybe a hobby that keeps you in shape for decades to come.

Shooting range. There's something compelling and empowering about holding, aiming, and squeezing the trigger of a Colt, Ruger, or Smith & Wesson. Local firing ranges have all the rules and will keep you safe. If a bride suggests this for her husband, I promise he will be blown away. Not literally.

The goal of all these things is to work up a little adrenaline and maybe a little sweat. Get those endorphins pumping and steal a kiss or a squeeze in the midst of all this physical activity. Everybody wins.[7]

— Question to Ask Out Loud —

There are close to 20 ideas sketched out above. Which one seems most doable in the next month or so?

"Don't sweat the petty things
and don't pet the sweaty things."

—GEORGE CARLIN

11

Couples Need…

To Do Stuff Slow and Easy

While the previous chapter had you sweating, this one has you chilling. But don't think the ideas below are just for people who are getting AARP applications in the mail. After all, the last chapter wasn't just for newlyweds.

The idea here is for all couples to take life down a notch and stop and smell the roses. Take a break from texts, deadlines, clients, bosses, classrooms, and time clocks. Just enjoy the experience. Be grateful. Together, remember. Hold hands and be friends again. Here are just a few ideas.

Concerts in the park. Within a short drive—or maybe in your own hometown—there's a downtown park that features summer concerts once a week. Or maybe a music festival that goes on for an entire week. The type of music isn't nearly as important as the atmosphere. Bring lawn chairs and join the other couples, families, and teenagers enjoying life. It's usually free.

Go back to high school. Even if you live far from your old alma mater, head over to your local high school for an occasional football game, choir concert, or theater production. There's a vibe on most high school campuses that gives you hope for the future.

Horse-drawn carriage. This is one of those things you've always wanted to do. Clip-clop through Central Park or around a small town square. Snuggle up and celebrate your life together.

Drive-in movie. According to nerve.com there are 338 drive-in movie locations remaining. On a clear summer night, find one. Maybe even watch the movie.[8]

Take the tour bus. For years, I dismissed the idea of sitting on a bus while some wannabe comedian squawked over a tinny microphone about who this building was named after or what happened a hundred years ago at this intersection. But Rita and I tried it once, and it gave us an entirely new appreciation for Chicago. Then we tried it again in Dublin while visiting our daughter, Rae Anne, at college. In one afternoon, you can see an entire downtown area, saving footsteps, energy, and cab fare.

Acquire some hard-to-get tickets. To a professional sporting event, rodeo, monster truck rally, symphony...or the reunion tour of your favorite rock band from high school. Something you'll talk about for years.

County fairs. Stay away from the rickety tilt-a-whirl. Stay away from the sticky, greasy, deep-fried elephant ears. But go ahead and waste ten bucks on the skills booths. You won't win anything. The rifle sights are bent, the basketball rim is oval, and the milk bottles are weighted and can't be knocked over. But it's still a hoot. The carnival barkers can be pretty entertaining as long as you keep your cool and keep your hand on your wallet.

Recreate your first date. Ask her out with the same hesitant words. Rent the same movie. Go to the same restaurant. Play the same music. Talk about the same topics. Relive the same awkward good-night kiss (or not).

Rent your dream car. If it's a Ferrari, Porsche, Jaguar, or classic Mustang, remember to watch your speed!

Art fairs. When the arts community takes over a park or shuts down a side street and erects a long row of tents, that's your cue to pretend you're art connoisseurs. Stand together at the entrance to each booth and nod thoughtfully. Point to a particular piece, whisper to each other, and again nod thoughtfully. Those nearby will think you're sophisticated dealers. Just don't stand too long at the velvet Elvis paintings.

Pack a picnic. Pick a summer Sunday afternoon. Or meet each other for a long lunch midweek. You can plan a gourmet brunch-in-a-basket days in advance or go to a local deli at the spur of the moment and ask for two box lunches to go. You already know the perfect grassy area to spread your blanket. It could be a local park, bustling with joggers and dog walkers. Or it could be an out-of-the-way strawberry patch or wooded glen that gives you all kinds of privacy.

Stay home and fake a power outage. No lights. No computers. No television. Get out the candles and…do stuff slow and easy.

— Question to Ask Out Loud —

When's the last time we strolled? Where might we stroll?

"Slow down and enjoy life.
It's not only the scenery you miss by going too fast—
you also miss the sense of where you are going and why."

—Eddie Cantor

12

Couples Need…

To See Marriage as Jesus Sees It

Feel free to question many of the philosophies, protocols, or social customs devised by humans. Arguments can be made for whether families, communities, or the federal government should be in charge of educating our kids. A generation ago, there were people who questioned the value of going to the moon when people were hungry here on earth. We could certainly debate the benefits of traveling sports teams for children under 12. How about paper versus plastic? Digital versus vinyl? Feel free to join the debate on the value of bike lanes, vaccines, online dating, term limits, and lawn fertilizer.

But do not even think about questioning the value of marriage.

Jesus never talked specifically about public schools, space exploration, or digital downloads, but when the Pharisees questioned him on the topic of marriage and divorce, he was quite clear. We referenced this passage in chapter 5, and it becomes even more compelling in context.

> "Haven't you read," [Jesus] replied, "that at the beginning the Creator 'made them male and female,' and said, 'For this reason a man will leave his father and mother and be united to his wife, and the two will become one flesh'? So they are no longer two, but one flesh. Therefore what God has joined together, let no one separate" (Matthew 19:4-6).

Jesus did acknowledge that marriage wasn't for everyone, but it's not something that should be devalued or dismissed. He even performed his first miracle at a marriage celebration. It would have been fascinating to watch the scene unfold. Fortunately, the second chapter of the Gospel of John describes that first-century slice of life from northern Israel.

A mother and her approximately 30-year-old son are attending a wedding. The mother is apparently a close friend or relative of the bride or groom because she shows concern when the weeklong celebration looks like it may be running out of wine. She tells her son about the problem, and while his initial statement suggests he doesn't want to be involved, being the good son, he does what needs to be done. You know the story.

> On the third day a wedding took place at Cana in Galilee. Jesus' mother was there, and Jesus and his disciples had also been invited to the wedding. When the wine was gone, Jesus' mother said to him, "They have no more wine."
>
> "Woman, why do you involve me?" Jesus replied. "My hour has not yet come."
>
> His mother said to the servants, "Do whatever he tells you."
>
> Nearby stood six stone water jars, the kind used by the Jews for ceremonial washing, each holding from twenty to thirty gallons.
>
> Jesus said to the servants, "Fill the jars with water"; so they filled them to the brim.
>
> Then he told them, "Now draw some out and take it to the master of the banquet."
>
> They did so, and the master of the banquet tasted the water that had been turned into wine. He did not realize where it had come from, though the servants who had drawn the water knew. Then he called the bridegroom aside and said, "Everyone brings out the choice wine first and then the cheaper wine after the guests have had too much to drink; but you have saved the best till now."
>
> What Jesus did here in Cana of Galilee was the first of the signs through which he revealed his glory; and his disciples believed in him (John 2:1-11).

Theologians love examining the subtext and meaning of this opening act of Jesus's earthly ministry. The takeaway for any bride and groom today is to make sure you have invited Jesus to the wedding ceremony *and* the marriage. Know that you can ask him for help when you run out of something...anything. Listen to his instructions. And expect to be wonderfully surprised.

Finally—and this is big—there is a sacred and divine aspect of holy wedlock that seems to have been lost in recent generations. Jesus even compared marriages to his own relationship with the Christian church: "Husbands, love your wives, just as Christ loved the church and gave himself up for her" (Ephesians 5:25).

Do you get that? The sacramental bond you have with your beloved reflects the relationship that God's Son has with those who have chosen to follow him. It's a love that goes beyond affection and romance. It's sacrificial. It's selfless. It's eternal.

— Question to Ask Out Loud —

Is Jesus in our marriage?

"There is no more lovely, friendly,
and charming relationship, communion,
or company than a good marriage."

—Martin Luther

13

Couples Need...

To Jab Less

For your reading pleasure and edification, I've come up with three lists of phrases, sentences, and concepts that should remain unspoken between husband and wife. Things he could say, she could say, and either of you could say—but shouldn't. Let's call them jabs.

Now, because you're human, you will *think* some of these things. Mean-spirited and anger-inducing jabs will come to mind, and sentences will even begin to form in your head.

The good news is, a biblical strategy to control your thought life is spelled out in Philippians 4:8: "Finally, brothers and sisters, whatever is true, whatever is noble, whatever is right, whatever is pure, whatever is lovely, whatever is admirable—if anything is excellent or praiseworthy—think about such things."

Intentionally taking control of your thought life is an ongoing and worthwhile goal. But this chapter suggests some instant changes you can make today simply by knowing what a jab is and realizing the damage it can do.

The best way to define the word "jab" is to give you a few real-life examples. See if you recognize any of these lines that might be tossed around in a marriage on the brink. He might say...

- "I'm thinking you wear a little too much makeup."
- "I'm thinking you need to wear a little more makeup."
- "Didn't we just have this same thing for dinner last week?"

- "What did you do all day?"

- "Did you see the new women's fitness center that just opened down the street?"

- "Actually, I'm not really hungry. I had a late lunch. I had to go over a proposal with Amber from marketing."

- "Did you really need another pair of shoes?"

- "My mom did it this way."

- "What did you do to your hair?"

- "So which is it tonight? Are you too tired, too distracted, or too crampy? Or do you just have your regular ten o'clock headache?"

- "What happened to your skinny jeans?"

- "How old was your mother when she started going gray?"

She might say...

- "I don't know how it happens, but the neighbors on both sides have zero dandelions."

- "You loaded the dishwasher wrong."

- "You're holding the baby wrong."

- "The Browns next door have a new car."

- "We were at their house last fall. His name is Mike. Her name is Carol. I wish you would remember the names of people I care about."

- "Leave it there. I'll have my brother come over and carry it upstairs."

- "Did you brush your teeth today?"

- "You're just like your father."

- "Didn't we just do it last week?"

- "We never go anywhere."

- "Forget it. I'll call someone. Or do it myself."

- "Sheila's husband just got another promotion."

Or either of you might say…

- "You knew I was like this when you married me."

- "You never, ever put the top back on the toothpaste. It's really unbelievable."

- "You know these mugs you bought don't fit in the dishwasher."

- "Two hundred channels, and this is what you're watching?"

- "Did you see what your son did? Why do you let him get away with that?"

- "I told you so."

- "Whatever."

- "What's wrong with you?"

- "Why can't you be more like…"

- "You always…"

- "You never…"

- "If you really loved me…"

Have any of these jabs been echoing through your kitchen or bedroom in the last week or so? These guaranteed squabble starters seem to come out of nowhere and tend to linger for a while.

But jabs do have a discernible, preventable pattern. Each one begins with an observation. It continues with a brief statement disguised to be helpful or informative. But it's not received that way and irritates instantly. In a flash, it grows from thought to spoken words to petty argument. Gone unchecked, that petty argument can easily escalate into a barrage of words and accusations that are not even true. That barrage of words and accusations can easily escalate into several days of silence and cold stares. Those days of silence and cold stares can easily escalate into threats of ripping the family apart. You've been warned. And if you think about it, you're really not surprised.

One final note. The most fascinating thing about jabs is that we know they're going to sting even before we say them. So why do we?

— Question to Ask Out Loud —

Which of the 36 jabs above are the most painful?

"Words from the mouth of a wise man are gracious,
while the lips of a fool consume him."

—ECCLESIASTES 10:12 NASB

14

Couples Need...

To Stroke More

Well, I guess since we spent the previous chapter detailing things not to say, we should probably consider a few phrases that can make married life a lot more fun—sometimes instantly. Let's call them strokes.

The warning here is that strokes need to be based on truth. Telling your wife, "This is the best stew I've ever had," is a significant problem if all she did was open a can of Dinty Moore or Campbell's Chunky Soup. Guys, you also need to know when your wife is feeling frumpy. You can always say, "I love you so much. You are so beautiful." But be careful using phrases like "You look fantastic" or "You and that dress...set phasers on stunning." Reserve over-the-top superlatives for those times when she has put in a little extra effort. Otherwise your well-meaning compliment will have the reverse effect.

Men are not quite as sensitive. We'll fall for a nice compliment anytime. But probably don't tell us you like our bald spot, paunch, or hairy back. We won't believe you, and we really don't like to be reminded of our physical shortcomings.

With those cautions, let's consider a few nice strokes. He might say...

- "I appreciate you."

- "You make me a better man."

- "I'm the luckiest guy in the world."

52

- "I'm proud of you."

- "You look great. That's one of my favorite outfits."

- "You have such great taste."

- "You and me. We can handle anything."

- "Sweets for the sweet."

- "You're the best mom in the world."

- "You make the best…"

- "I must have thought about you a hundred times today."

- "You take my breath away."

She might say…

- "I'm glad I married you."

- "You're a great dad."

- "Thanks for taking care of me."

- "Can you open this jar for me?"

- "Thanks for last night."

- "You are one handsome man."

- "Kiss me."

- "I trust you."

- "Can you scrub my back?"

- "Can I sit in your lap?"

- "The kids are spending the night at Grandma's."

- "I love my life."

Or either of you might say…

- "You make me smile."

- "You're the best."

- "You're my best friend."

- "Thanks."

- "Just want you to know I'll be praying for you."

- "You're awesome. I don't deserve you."

- "You, me, and God. It's going to be okay."

- "You rock my world."

- "I love your laugh."

- "What would I do without you?"

- "There's no one I'd rather grow old with than you."

- "I love you."

Words are powerful. The memory of something you said to your beloved years ago can still bring smiles. I trust you and your beloved have shared some of these phrases with each other.

The above list is really quite incomplete. It should be customized based on your history and circumstance.

If she's nervous about going to take the bar exam, don't just wish her luck. Tell her how much you love her and how she's your hero.

If he just missed out on a promotion, tell him you have faith in him and he's a great husband. Let him know that even though he had a bad day, he's given you a wonderful life. Extra kisses don't hurt either.

Worth noting. Strokes like these can be spoken, texted, slipped into briefcases, written on steamy mirrors, and whispered in crowded rooms.

One final note. The most fascinating thing about strokes is that we know our beloved loves to hear them. So why don't we say the things we know will bring joy to their day?

— Question to Ask Out Loud —

Which of the 36 strokes would you appreciate most?

"How do I love thee? Let me count the ways.
I love thee to the depth and breadth and height
My soul can reach."

—Elizabeth Barrett Browning

15

Couples Need...

To Prayer Walk

Dave and Geri take walks several times a week. Sometimes they spend the entire walk talking. To God.

Prayer walks have become a fascinating and compelling point of connection for their marriage. They don't remember exactly how it began, but they have been prayer walking for years and often consider each walk to be the highlight of their day.

The rules are loose. And the pressure to "do it right" is zero. They happen to live in a neighborhood with lots of sidewalks, not far from paved walking paths along the Fox River. They walk after dinner, on weekend afternoons, and even sometimes early in the morning. The route changes. The topics change. And the intensity of the prayer changes depending on what's going on in their lives and the lives of their family and friends.

It's not a secret. The kids know that Mom and Dad pray while they walk together. On a rare occasion, one of their kids will even join them. Dave and Geri don't announce, "We're going on a prayer walk now!" But when Mom and Dad head out the door in walking shoes, dressed for the weather, there's a sense that all is right with the world. Over the next half hour or so, the needs of the family are going to be lifted and turned over to God. That's always a good thing.

Every walk is different. Before, during, and after their extended prayer, Dave and Geri talk to each other—especially when there's something relevant in the moment. "Check out that squirrel." "Watch out for that dog poop." "We may need to take the short path—I promised Sam we'd go shopping for shoes later."

But most of the talking is done out loud with God. Sometimes they focus on a single concern for the entire walk and pray with an alarming intensity. More often, it's a potpourri of topics reflecting the diversity and busyness of suburban family life. On some walks, he will do most of the praying. Sometimes she does. Often they go back and forth, one person picking up where the other leaves off. As you can imagine, it is a wonderfully unifying process.

Again, there are no hard-and-fast rules to prayer walking. Dave and Geri laugh that sometimes a prayer request to God simultaneously conveys new information to the other person. That's not the goal, but sometimes it just happens. For instance, Geri might initiate prayer for a young couple who just got engaged, which informs Dave to save the date. Dave might spill his heart to God concerning a situation at work, and that gives Geri fresh insight about why her husband might be feeling extra stressed and might need a bit more patience from her.

Of course, prayer is all about focusing on and communicating with the Creator of the universe, not coordinating schedules with your spouse. While God definitely deserves our undivided attention, I think he honors the way Dave and Geri multitask while they pray.

One of the other great values of prayer walking is that silence is really okay. If a couple were to sit down at the kitchen table with the intention of praying, any lengthy silence might be awkward. But Geri and Dave might cover two or three blocks without a sound. Those minutes are also immeasurably valuable.

Best of all is the way this couple has invited God into their marriage. He continues to empower them to do great things for the kingdom. I can't wait to see how their next ministry assignment unfolds. I'm a little jealous.

— Question to Ask Out Loud —

Ready to walk?

"So be careful to do what the LORD your God has commanded you; do not turn aside to the right or to the left. Walk in obedience to all that the LORD your God has commanded you, so that you may live and prosper and prolong your days in the land that you will possess."

—DEUTERONOMY 5:32-33

16

Couples Need…

To Hit Bottom Together

Has your marriage hit bottom? Have you reached a point where the two of you realized things could no longer go the way they were going? It may be after some dramatic event that makes newspaper headlines. Or it could be a quiet crushing moment in a small suburban bungalow. Most couples have at least one moment that makes or breaks their marriage.

When it happens in your marriage, please make sure the two of you fall together down into the darkness of the abyss. If one of you stands at the top of the pit, mocking or blaming or denying any responsibility, then your wedding vows were a deceit, merely for show. But if you hit bottom together, both of you will be there with no choice but to reach toward, lift up, boost, and support each other as you crawl out into the sun.

By the way, there's a very good chance that God has allowed you to fall. But don't be angry with him, because he is also the One who pulls you out to set your feet on solid rock.

A story might help you understand this principle.

Once upon a time a boy named Jay was full of optimism and potential. Plus he was kinda cute, so Rita said yes when Jay got on one knee and presented her with a huge one-quarter-carat diamond ring. The fact that he had not achieved much didn't matter because his new wife had a lot of faith in her young husband.

Until she didn't.

You see, before long Jay and Rita had two small boys and were a couple months behind in their FHA mortgage. Silly Jay was trying to earn a living selling law books to corporate attorneys, and he was not very good at it. He slogged around the Chicago loop carrying a 26-pound briefcase filled with samples. His three polyester three-piece suits were getting shabbier and shabbier. His lone pair of black wingtips that once belonged to his grandfather had holes in their soles. Every month, he got further and further behind in his sales quotas.

Still, even in the midst of the job angst, Jay and Rita's life was not all bad. Their two boys were healthy and smart. The family was plugged in to a good church and even had friends praying for them. Every evening, Rita kissed her husband and asked about his day. That was a good thing. And sometimes a hard thing.

Here, it's worth pointing out that guys' identity and self-esteem are often wrapped up in the success they experience on the job. Maybe that shouldn't be the case, but it is.

Not surprisingly, Jay's optimism was disappearing. His potential seemed nowhere to be found. The world Jay had once hoped to conquer was beating him up and dragging him down. Rita still loved him. Which is why she did what she did.

She could have screamed at Jay to work harder. She could have pretended everything was okay. She could have taken the two boys and moved home to her mom and dad's house. She could have complained to all her friends and made his life miserable until he moved out.

Instead, she spoke. Rita did not raise her voice. She did not accuse. As she sat on the floor of their tiny living room, she looked at her husband standing in the kitchen doorway and said, "I don't have faith in you anymore."

It hurt Jay to hear that. But somehow, they were exactly the right words at exactly the right time. Rita was telling Jay he was not alone. They were partners, and they needed to face any crisis with honesty, commitment, and communication. As he stood in the doorway, Jay experienced the worst and best moment of his life.

No, he didn't become a better salesman. That would have been impossible. But Jay did write those seven words on a three-by-five card and pushpin it on the wall above his desk: *"I don't have faith in you anymore."* Jay stopped feeling sorry for himself. He hustled a little more. He reevaluated his gifts, passions, and career options. Jay and Rita intentionally spent more time talking about goals, hopes, dreams, and God's plan for their lives.

That summer, Jay changed careers. His first job as an entry-level copywriter at a small advertising agency on Michigan Avenue was a direct result of those husband-and-wife talks about all the things that really matter. When Jay told Rita the new job would actually reduce their income, she didn't hesitate. The young mother proved once again that she knew her husband and knew exactly what he needed to hear. Rita said, "We'll make it work."

Thirty years later, Jay still can't sell anything. But the bills are getting paid, their four sons have college degrees, their daughter is finishing college as well, four daughters-in-law have joined the family, as well as four perfect grandchildren. No one has missed a meal. And Rita and Jay have one more little joke that gets sprinkled into their current conversations about goals, hopes, dreams, and God's plan for their lives. Jay will say, "Do you have faith in me?" And Rita gets a twinkle in her eye and says, "For now."

And they lived happily ever after.[9]

— Question to Ask Out Loud —

Are we on this roller coaster of life together? Are we committed to sharing the ups and downs? Is there something quiet and heartfelt we need to say so we're in the same place?

"More marriages might survive if the partners realized that sometimes the better comes after the worse."

—Doug Larson

17

Couples Need...

To Help Each Other Find Answers

My kids grew up with the annual ritual of watching *It's a Wonderful Life* every Christmas season. We can mimic quite a few of the scenes word for word, sometimes in a pretty accurate Jimmy Stewart stammer. The 1946 film is jam-packed with life lessons, including at least one on how to connect as a couple. If you're a fan, this chapter will make a lot more sense. If not, see if you can follow along anyway.

Let's take a look at the scene in which George Bailey has just found out that his brother, Harry, is engaged and won't be able to take over at the Bailey Brothers Building and Loan. Suddenly, George realizes he is forever stuck in Bedford Falls. But his mom has a plan. She knows that Mary Hatch—the level-headed, wholesome girl down the street— is smitten with George and vice versa.

```
EXTERIOR BAILEY HOME AT NIGHT
MEDIUM CLOSE SHOT

George is standing at the garden gate. He
takes some travel folders from his pocket,
looks at them, and throws them away. He is
obviously disturbed about the latest turn of
events. His mother comes out of the house and
kisses him.
```

                    GEORGE
    Hello, Mom.

        MRS. BAILEY (As she kisses him)
        That's for nothing. How do you like
    her?

She nods toward the house, where Harry
and Ruth can be seen through the front door
dancing with a crowd of other couples to the
MUSIC of a phonograph.

                    GEORGE
    She's swell.

                MRS. BAILEY
        Looks like she can keep Harry on his
    toes.

                    GEORGE
    Keep him out of Bedford Falls, anyway.

                MRS. BAILEY
        Did you know that Mary Hatch is back
    from school?

                    GEORGE
    Uh-huh.

                MRS. BAILEY
    Came back three days ago.

                    GEORGE
    Hmm...

                MRS. BAILEY
    Nice girl, Mary.

                    GEORGE
         Hmm...

                    MRS. BAILEY
         Kind that will help you find the answers,
         George.

                    GEORGE
         Hmm...

                    MRS. BAILEY
         Oh, stop that grunting.

                    GEORGE
         Hmm...

If you know the movie, you know the next scene. George begrudgingly goes to Mary's house. At first she's excited to see him. They say some not-so-nice things to each other. George leaves, and in frustration Mary smashes the record "Buffalo Gals." Sam Wainwright calls. George comes back for his hat and gives an ultimatum. The scene ends with George and Mary kissing passionately, and then it abruptly cuts to the newlyweds leaving the wedding chapel.

All because Mrs. Bailey saw something in Mary and spoke from the heart. "Kind that will help you find the answers, George." For the rest of the movie, Mary does exactly that. She gives George their entire honeymoon fund to help save the building and loan. With the help of Bert the cop and Ernie the cabdriver, she turns the leaky old Granville house into a honeymoon suite. She becomes a supportive partner in his business, turns the dilapidated house into a home, and raises their kids to be respectful and appreciative. Best of all, Mary initiates the chain of prayer when she sees her husband has hit bottom. (You'll recall that the first eight lines of the movie are prayers for George.)

Mary helps her husband find the answers. She chooses old mossback George over the millionaire Sam Wainwright. But she doesn't rub his nose in it. She makes her husband a better man. Does that describe your marriage relationship?

The problem with this kind of question (and this chapter) is that you might be saying, "My wife (or husband) doesn't help me like that!" Or, "I don't get answers from my husband (or wife). All I get are orders." Those kinds of thoughts will have some discontented women and men thinking about trading their spouse in for a newer, more helpful model.

I hope you know where this is going. Our thoughts should not be accusations aimed at our spouse. We should be asking ourselves, *Am I the kind of companion that helps my spouse find the answers?*

Consider this. Every day, your husband or wife gets out of bed with a headful of questions. Some will be answered that day. Some require a lifetime to answer. Questions that range from *What's the weather today?* to *What's the meaning of life?*

That's where this chapter will end. With apologies to readers who glazed over because they're unfamiliar with the Frank Capra classic.

Still, don't miss this point. Your spouse has questions. Your role is not so much to *give* each other answers, but to come alongside and help each other *find* the answers. Know the difference, and you, too, can have a wonderful life.

— Question to Ask Out Loud —

Right now in our marriage, what are our most urgent questions?

"Remember the night we broke the windows in this old house? This is what I wished for."

—MARY HATCH (DONNA REED),
IT'S A WONDERFUL LIFE

18

Couples Need...

To Keep It Clean

Chances are that having a spic-and-span home is more important to one of you than to the other.

In the Payleitner home, that would most definitely be Rita. She can't go to bed with dishes in the sink. She's also much more likely to enjoy a vacation or long weekend if the carpets back home have been vacuumed. (That's right. *No one* is in the house, but for some reason she needs the carpets to be dirt-free.) My wonderful bride is also just a bit fanatic about clearing the morning newspaper from the kitchen table. Sometimes while I'm still reading it. Finally, she goes through Fantastic, Formula 409, and Windex like it's her job. Where I might use one squirt, she pulls that trigger six or eight times.

Rita would never be labeled a neat freak. But she's neater than me in quite a few departments.

Well, much to my regret and embarrassment, I need to say...she's right and I'm wrong. When it comes to minimizing stress and increasing productivity, clean is most definitely better. Organized is better. Decluttering your life is a good idea. Sorry if that doesn't go over well with you. But it's just true.

The bonus is that being cleaner and decluttered also leads to better sex. Have I got your attention now?

A recent survey sponsored by Liquid-Plumr interviewed women about the connection between a clean house and romance. One-third of respondents admitted to fantasizing about their significant other while doing housework. And 49 percent of women who took the survey said they were more likely to be intimate after chores had been completed.[10]

If you think about it for just a minute, that shouldn't be surprising. Sure, Hollywood might occasionally present a hot and sweaty couple enjoying some raw primal passion. After working together in the garden on a Saturday afternoon, you and your spouse may find yourselves oddly attracted to each other with dirt on your foreheads and sweat dripping down your cheeks. But those are the exceptions to the rule.

A tidy master bedroom with freshly laundered sheets, dust-free dressers, and no dirty socks on the floor has a much better chance of becoming a love nest. Maybe that's one of the reasons why hotel romance is so well received. Sure you're on vacation. Sure you've escaped the daily routine. Sure the kids are miles away. But really, it's all about the clean.

Men, take note. You know how it's impossible to hold a conversation with your wife when you're watching your hometown team attempting a comeback in overtime? Well, your bride probably can't fully focus on lovemaking if there are smelly workout clothes piled outside the closet door, used tissues on the floor next to the wastebasket, and a stained coffee cup on the nightstand. Are you writing this down?

Ladies, as gatekeepers when it comes to romance, note this warning. You may be tempted to use this information as a weapon or tool to get your way. Please don't. "We can't make love because the dining room needs to be dusted," doesn't feel like a valid statement. Maybe even worse, "If you scrub the bathroom, we can have sex." That's dangerous ground.

So guys and gals, if you're looking to spice things up, instead of investing in a weekend away, consider spending that same amount of money on maid service. Or even better, maybe the two of you could spend 45 minutes of foreplay with dust rags and a vacuum cleaner, folding laundry, filling laundry baskets, wiping down sinks and mirrors, and changing the sheets and pillowcases. Let me know how that works out, and maybe I'll suggest it to my bride.

It's not in the Bible, but there's still some truth to it—cleanliness is next to godliness.

— Question to Ask Out Loud —

If you could make one of my dirty habits go away, what would it be? (Be gentle.)

"I hate housework! You make the beds,
you do the dishes, and six months later you have
to start all over again."

—Joan Rivers

19

Couples Need…

To Admit You're Different and Be Glad

This book—including this chapter—was written by a guy. So please forgive me for my pathetic attempt to explain how men are different from women. You will soon discover the list below perpetuates several stereotypes and myths. (All of which just happen to be true.)

- Men like *The Three Stooges*. Women are Stooge haters.

- Men look at a color swatch and say blue. Women look at the same color swatch and say periwinkle or navy or turquoise or teal or cobalt.

- Women are always ready to share their thoughts and feelings, sometimes with tears. Men grunt.

- Women love chocolate. Men (smart ones) buy it for them.

- Women love children. Men sometimes acknowledge the existence of short people living in the house.

- Women expect men to change. Men don't change.

- Men claim that the first thing they notice about a woman is her eyes. Women know that's a lie.

- Some men look good in a moustache. No woman looks good in a moustache.

- Women dot their *i*'s with hearts and end handwritten notes with smiley faces. Men don't use pens or pencils anymore.

- Women look in the mirror and hate what they see. Men look in the mirror, suck in their gut, flex, and say, "Not bad…not bad at all" or "Still got it." Even if they never had it.

- Men's brains are 12 percent bigger than women's brains. Enough said.

- Women are embarrassed by flatulence. Men are amused by flatulence.

- Men own 3 pairs of shoes. Women own between 4 and 400 pairs.

- Men's haircuts cost $13. Plus a $2 tip. Women's haircuts cost $75. Plus a $10 tip.

- Women make their beds in hotels. Men don't know why women do this.

- Women feel empowered through emotional support by a loving husband. Men feel empowered by a full tank of gas and $300 in their wallet.

- Women pile things at the bottom of the stairs as a reminder to take them up on the next trip. Men step over those things.

- Men forget birthdays and anniversaries. Women should accept this fact by now.

Did you laugh? Don't feel guilty. Like most humor, the stereotypes are funny because they contain a kernel of truth. Maybe you even learned something about each other.

Which brings us to the real purpose of this chapter. Let's admit that guys and gals are also quite different in their attitude about sex. You already know this. But it's good to get this kind of thing out in the open.

Guys can be ready for romance at a moment's notice. That's how God made us—ready, willing, and able after we see a TV commercial for auto parts or hear elevator music of a pretty bad song from the '80s. I confess that sometimes thoughts about having sex with my bride can be triggered unexpectedly in the middle of a busy workday by the mere mention of a particular city, car, artist, movie, style of shirt, candy bar, candle scent, or season of the year. (The list is actually longer than that, but something distracted me from completing it.) I even remember one time a typo left a provocative word on my laptop and I lost focus for the rest of the afternoon, causing me to miss an editor's deadline. Blame love.

While husbands can be ready in a moment's notice, wives can be derailed from sex just as quickly. You know the scenario. Maybe it's date night. Maybe it's a special occasion planned months in advance. Maybe it's a late-night rendezvous you agreed to that morning, and the anticipation of it kept both of you smiling all day long. You even texted each other slightly naughty emojis during lunch. He's ready. She's just about ready. It's go time. But all that momentum and potential can be lost in an instant. How? The list is endless.

Your baby cries. Your third grader pukes. Your high schooler stomps around the house looking for his cell phone charger. Your college student calls about her schizophrenic roommate. The furnace makes a funny noise. Her mother calls to ask about Thanksgiving. Her mother doesn't call to ask about Thanksgiving. The late local news has a story about a lost dog that looks like her dog when she was little.

These are all potential deal breakers. None of them are his fault. Most of them couldn't possibly be predicted or prevented.

On the other hand, sometimes it *is* his fault. Maybe he did something to spoil her mood. He mentioned the pot roast was a little dry. He said something about the new receptionist at work. He left the sprinkler on too long after she just finished talking about the higher-than-usual utility bill. He belched on his way to the bathroom. He left his socks on the floor.

The evening is derailed. Both he and she feel bad about the missed opportunity. And maybe, if you both admit it—and laugh about it—the night can still be rescued. Knowing how to deflect distractions and reignite passion are all part of the game we call married life. Learn the rules, and you've got a better chance of winning.

Veteran husbands have learned this game strategy: Be proactive setting the stage for a successful attempt at lovemaking. They tuck the little ones in themselves to make sure they are fast asleep. They do a sweep of the master bedroom to make sure nothing assaults the senses—extreme temperatures, dirty towels, peculiar smells, a stack of unpaid bills, or toothpaste in the sink. They offer a cup of herbal tea, glass of ice water, or some other nightcap to ensure their bride's comfort at the end of the day. They brush their teeth. They lock the bedroom door, lest the rug rats invade. They may even light a scented candle.

Ladies, we know we are at your mercy. In most marriages, men are the initiators and women are the gatekeepers in this arena. And that's okay.

In a way, her sensitive nature and her need to have everything just right prevents a husband from taking his bride for granted. When he does get the green light, an experienced husband knows how to make the very best of it. He takes his time. He hits all the right spots. He makes the most of the opportunity. And his wife appreciates the extra effort.

It's nice to be appreciated.

— Question to Ask Out Loud —

What can we do to better establish the mood and set the tone for a nice night of romance?

"God made man and then said, 'I can do better than that,' and made woman."

—ADELA ROGERS ST. JOHNS

20

Couples Need…

To Rescue Humanity

You don't litter. You don't leave puppies in hot cars. You recycle pop cans, cereal boxes, and jelly jars. You donate old dishes and dish towels to Goodwill. You switched most of your incandescent light bulbs to LEDs, CFLs, or halogens. You even help little old ladies across the street.

Those things are all very nice and thoughtful. But probably the most helpful thing you've ever done for the world was to get hitched.

In chapter 7 we explored some of the many ways healthy marriages lead to well-adjusted children. But there are tons of other benefits as well. By getting married and staying married, you help reduce chronic illness and stress in the workplace.[11] You increase the economic well-being of your community. You reduce the incidents of depression and alcoholism. You lower the death rate.

Married people even volunteer more. You may have the image of a pack of good-looking young do-gooders sorting canned goods, picking up trash, whitewashing fences, and spreading mulch for the common good. But my hunch is those kids are probably doing those things so they can list them on their college application or maybe to flirt with other good-looking young do-gooders. The truth is, married adults are 1.3 times more likely to volunteer for social services and average 1.4 times more volunteer hours.[12]

The impact of strong marriages extends further than you may have ever considered. Marriages and families are the building blocks of neighborhoods, communities, and countries. Don't let that idea crush you with the burden of responsibility. Really, it should ennoble you with purpose and potential.

Despite the obvious benefits, please be aware that marriage is an institution under attack. The culture and even some of our laws undermine the marriage relationship. In many circles, divorce is presented as an easy alternative with little or no regard for the fallout. You may know couples who see marriage as disposable and are contacting divorce attorneys. It's tempting to take his side or her side, but it's more productive to cement your own relationship and model the value of a lifelong commitment.

So, yeah. Marriage is just about the best thing you've got going. Whether you're scheduled to walk down the aisle later this year or celebrating multiple decades of wedded bliss, don't disparage marriage. It's a gift. It's a goal. There's a virtual guarantee that your life is going to turn out better with a spouse than without one.

So celebrate your marriage. Every chance you get.

— Question to Ask Out Loud —

What's the best part about being married?

---

*"Therefore what God has joined together,
let no one separate."*

—MARK 10:9

21

Couples Need…

To Identify a Couple Go-To Couples

This happens to you a few times every year.

You hear about an event that sounds like great fun. Maybe it's something you see online, hear on the radio, read in the newspaper, see on a marquee, or just happen to stumble over in the course of life.

It could be anything. A slam poetry reading. A midnight showing of a classic movie. A restaurant ribbon cutting. A reunion tour of a band you followed in your youth. A charity sporting event. A tractor pull. A book signing by a favorite author. An ice-sculpting competition. A political rally. An art auction. You get the idea.

It's something you would love to do, and you instantly think of the perfect couple to do it with. Joe and Lori! They're about your age, and you've been wanting to connect with them. Good sense of humor. Smart, cool, fun. He's not a blowhard. She's not a nag.

It's the perfect double date. But there's one problem. The event is tonight. (Or maybe tomorrow night.)

Do you call them up? Well, let's consider your thought process…

What a blast it would be to do this! It's too bad we didn't hear about this a few weeks ago. Attending this event with Joe and Lori would have truly been a highlight of the year. We can't call them now because it's too late. They're probably busy. And even if they aren't busy, they'll be insulted because we apparently think they have nothing better to do than sit around and wait for a phone call. Or they may say yes just to be nice, and we certainly don't want them to do this if they don't want to. And if they really are busy and they say no it will be awkward next time we see them because they'll feel bad for saying no. Even worse they'll think we're calling them at the last minute because someone else canceled or they were our last choice when really they were our first.

So do you call or text Joe and Lori? Probably not. And really, it's okay. It's not the end of the world. The two of you might go to the event anyway and have a swell time. But for the entire evening you will both be thinking that it could have been sweller. Which takes a bit of the luster off the event.

Worse, maybe you *don't* go, and there's a twinge of regret and even a little totally unreasonable anger directed at Joe and Lori because *you* felt as if you couldn't call them. The ultimate twist of irony would be that they also heard about the same event but didn't call you for the same reason.

How can you prevent such an agonizing chain of events? More importantly, how can you set yourself up so you have a great time and make great memories with Joe and Lori next time the opportunity arises?

Consider asking them if they'd like to be one of your go-to couples. What's that? Well, it's another married couple you can call at the last minute with no expectation and no hard feelings. If they're too tired, already booked, or don't even answer their phone, it's 100 percent okay. Hopefully, you will become a go-to couple for them as well so they feel comfortable calling you with an amazing last-minute idea that leads to a magical double date.

The best way to secure such a relationship is first to test your compatibility. The four of you should probably do something planned well in advance. Go online and find an event a couple months out. Something that requires tickets—a non-raunchy comedian coming to the area, a concert, a professional sporting event…something you already suspect may be of mutual interest to all involved. Then—just like high school—ask them out. If you feel daring, you can purchase four tickets and then start looking for the right couple. Or ask Joe and Lori if they're interested and then set the date and buy the tickets.

If all goes well, wait a few weeks and then have this conversation:

"Hey, we were thinking about you guys the other night. After a busy week, we suddenly found ourselves free on Saturday evening. So we almost called you guys to see if you wanted to do something. But it was already five o'clock, and we thought that was too last-minute, or insulting, or just bad etiquette. So we didn't call. Then we started wondering whether that would have been okay to call. What do you think?"

If they respond affirmatively, you have your answer. Let them know they can also call you anytime spontaneously. If they're confused or balk at the idea of impulse outings, keep them on your list of couples that need longer notice.

Last thoughts on go-to couples. You can certainly have more than one couple that falls in this category. Don't overlook family members, including siblings and cousins. If they turn down your last-minute invitation three or four times in a row, don't take it personally. They might simply be in a busy season of life. Maybe go back to long-range date planning with them.

Good luck. Don't put too much pressure on yourself or your friends. Ultimately, the goal is to elevate your marriage and theirs.

— Question to Ask Out Loud —

When was the last time we were on a double date? What married (or engaged) couples do we know that might be up for an evening out?

"Friendship is unnecessary, like philosophy, like art, like the universe itself (for God did not need to create). It has no survival value; rather it is one of those things which give value to survival."

—C.S. Lewis

22

Couples Need...

To Read Ephesians 5:22 in Context

Occasionally, you might run across some boorish oaf who believes Ephesians 5:22 is about keeping a woman in a subservient role, insisting her opinion has no value, and limiting her contribution to cooking, cleaning, and being available to his sexual whims.

That's what happens when you pluck a few words out of Scripture without seeing the bigger picture. It's true the verse clearly states, "Wives, submit to your own husbands as you do to the Lord." But thoughtful consideration of surrounding verses reveals a lesson that goes far beyond household duties.

Let's begin with the nine words immediately preceding that verse. Ephesians 5:21 says quite plainly, "Submit to one another out of reverence for Christ." That expands the idea of submission, doesn't it? The apostle Paul was writing to believers in the church at Ephesus and all believers everywhere. We are all expected to have the heart of a servant and put others' needs first.

Then Paul gives three real-life applications. Because strong families are the building blocks of a society, he begins by relating how submission works for wives, husbands, and kids. It's all about meeting each other's needs. Men need to lead. Women need to feel cherished. Children need instruction. Read it for yourself.

> Wives, submit to your own husbands as you do to the
> Lord. For the husband is the head of the wife as Christ

is the head of the church, his body, of which he is the Savior... (5:22-23).

Husbands, love your wives, just as Christ loved the church and gave himself up for her... In this same way, husbands ought to love their wives as their own bodies. He who loves his wife loves himself... (5:25,28).

Children, obey your parents in the Lord, for this is right (6:1).

Husbands, did you hear your marching orders? Your wife needs you to take a leadership role. But you need to lead with love. Sacrificial love. Just as Christ gave his life for us, men need to willingly give their lives for their brides.

Now some men are thinking, *I can do that. I would certainly rescue my wife from a rampaging warthog or do battle with a ninja assassin.* Sorry, guys—if only it were that easy. Those exciting scenarios are probably not going to happen, so you need to think in terms of sacrificing something much more mundane. Loving your wife sacrificially means putting her well-being before your own when it comes to your time, energy, resources, creativity, and even your will. That's right. You lead... for her sake.

If she's unhappy, suffering, discouraged, ignored, or feeling unloved, there's a problem. Like any good leader, you need to set aside your own needs until her needs are met.

Wives, if your husband is doing his part, your part shouldn't be difficult at all. Show him recognition and respect for leading the family. If you belittle his words and ignore his leadership, the entire family will surely suffer. A wise woman will not only respect her husband but also help him gain respect from others. In a positive way—by coming alongside as his advocate and also by never participating in the popular sport of husband bashing.

Look again at Ephesians 5:21. "Submit to one another out of reverence for Christ."

Some theologians call it mutual submission. Others don't like that term, but it's a pretty accurate paraphrase of how the Bible describes a successful marriage. He sacrifices. She submits. Both are looking for the best in each other and looking out for each other.

For the record, nowhere does the Bible tell women, "Obey your husbands." "Love, honor, and obey" were once part of the wedding vows, but you won't hear that at many of today's wedding ceremonies.

The word "obey" is saved for the kids. This is good news. Ephesians 6:1 confirms it's still okay for Mom and Dad to expect obedience from the next generation.

That three-part plan is one more example of how God designed families and cares about your marriage. He didn't just leave you to flounder without guidance. As Creator, he is well aware that men and women are different. I hope you're glad about that.

— Question to Ask Out Loud —

(She asks him:) What makes you feel respected?
(He asks her:) What makes you feel cherished?

"There is nothing more admirable than two people who see eye-to-eye keeping house as man and wife, confounding their enemies, and delighting their friends."

—Homer

23

Couples Need...

To Connect Despite the Kids

One of the oldest running jokes in the world is how kids put a halt to romance. And believe me, I get the joke.

The distraction and prohibition begin with the last trimester of your first pregnancy and end when your youngest child leaves home. That's very likely more than a couple decades.

What you need is a plan. A plan for making time for romance even though you're both a little tired, you're both a little distracted, and all your extra cash is already going for disposable diapers, book fees, field trips, piano lessons, braces, college funds, and so on. The little darlings are worth every nickel, but the budget for weekend getaways to Jamaica has dwindled considerably.

So how might you connect (or reconnect) with your coparenting partner on a regular basis without adding even more stress to the bank account or calendar?

Meet for lunch. Evenings can be crazy. Homework, after-school activities, bedtime rituals...maybe you don't think of lunch as a date, but it can be.

Take a day off during the school year. If all your kids are in school, schedule a vacation day for just the two of you on a Monday, Tuesday, Wednesday, Thursday, or Friday. It doesn't matter what you do. You could even do *nothing*. Culture says moms and dads need to save vacation days for family time. But wouldn't an occasional day off as a couple be a blessing to your entire family?

Hire a babysitter. But instead of going out as a couple, pay for the sitter to take the kids to a movie or some other outing. Wouldn't that be nice? A quiet evening in your own home…mmm.

Drop the kids at church. Lots of churches schedule activities for students from kindergarten through high school on Wednesday nights. When I speak to dads, I challenge them to volunteer at those events with the goal of connecting with their kids. But talking to couples, I would say *don't* volunteer. One parent could drop off the kids while the other prepares a nice dinner at home. Or both parents drop off the kids and continue down the road for a two-hour kid-free outing. Just remember to pick 'em up.

Do the Disney distraction. Bring home a pizza and pop and a kid-friendly movie. Suddenly Mom and Dad have at least 90 minutes of free time to chat, plan the family vacation, do taxes, or anything else you can think of.

Watch your friends' kids. If their kids get along with your kids, it's a win-win. But the best news is that next week, your friends will watch *your* kids.

Call Grandma. Ask her to watch the kids because you need some "quality time" as a couple. Go ahead and use air quotes. She'll chuckle—and be delighted to help!

Catch a cat nap. The idea of postponing romance until the kids are asleep is impractical and exhausting. Babies wake you anytime, day or night. School-age kids get tucked in at nine, but they may have a bad dream or need a glass of water in the middle of the night. Teens may come in after midnight. So squeeze in naps when you can. If Mom sneaks away for a 20-minute snooze after supper, the kids may not even miss her. But that may provide her with a bit of energy when the house finally quiets down.

Make your master bedroom a haven. If it seems like the redecorating budget goes toward the kids' rooms and communal living space, redirect some of those funds to the master bedroom. A fresh coat of paint. Some nice art. Mood lighting. Window blinds. Most importantly, a door lock that works. If you have a master bathroom, count yourself fortunate and use that shower or tub creatively.

Kids should bring you closer. Don't allow their needs to pull you apart. You need time together to be the kind of parents God is calling you to be. So find time for long conversations and even longer romantic interludes. Or even just to go to a movie and hold hands. Your time together doesn't have to break the bank. But do keep saving for that weekend jaunt to Jamaica.

— Question to Ask Out Loud —

Which of the strategies above might help us find some quiet time together in the next four days?

"My wife and I have the secret to making a marriage last. Two times a week we go to a nice restaurant. A little wine, good food…she goes Tuesdays, I go Fridays."

—HENNY YOUNGMAN

24

Couples Need...

To Connect Because of the Kids

The last chapter may have seemed to suggest that kids have a negative impact on a marriage. I know firsthand the opposite is true. Perhaps the times I feel closest and most connected with Rita are when we are sitting in church with our family between us. One kid, five kids, or the whole crew, including grandkids.

Raising awesome kids—if God has called you to parenthood—is a worthy goal. It can motivate husbands and wives to work together, and it gives you a shared vision of the future.

You've heard the running joke about a man and woman out for an intimate dinner, but the only thing they talk about is the kids. TV and movie screenwriters think it's hilarious—a married couple is out for a romantic candlelit dinner, and just as they begin to look into each other's eyes, the mood is broken by a call from the kids asking where to order the pizza or who is supposed to take out the garbage.

Well, that's not exactly sidesplitting, but it does bring up a question worth considering. Is it acceptable for a husband and wife to spend an evening out on a date—with no children in sight—and spend the entire time talking about the kids?

The answer is...that's a stupid question. A couple can talk about whatever they want as long as it's engaging and interesting to both him and her.

If you share a fascination with opera or monster trucks or seventeenth-century Italian tapestries, then chat away. But don't feel guilty for talking about what's going on in the lives of each of your kids. After all, it's a topic of conversation that's compelling to both of you.

You could certainly agree before your romantic dinner to limit yourself to topics that do not involve diapers, tucking in, birthday parties, back-to-school night, report cards, soccer carpools, piano lessons, or anything to do with the children. But that might leave one of you prattling on while the other smiles and nods politely. Does she really care that the wide receiver on his fantasy football team sprained an ankle? Does he really care about the color of the bridesmaids' dresses at her cousin's wedding?

For sure, the two of you care about every significant detail of each other's daily life. Here's a good rule of thumb: If it's important to your spouse, it's important to you. If one of you needs some encouragement or advice on a non-family-related topic, then make time for that conversation. In other words, every conversation doesn't have to be about the kids.

But you must admit, when one of you has new insight about what's going on in the lives of your kids—no matter how old they are—the conversation flows. You absolutely want details about any new milestones for your toddler. You care desperately about your son's run-in with the schoolyard bully and your daughter's college search. You're eager to hear the result of your sophomore's audition for the spring musical or tryout for basketball.

As a committed mother and father, it's rewarding and purposeful to compare notes on the gifts and talents you see developing in your kids—and even the challenges they face. Together, you celebrate your children's successes. Together, you help each other gain perspective on their setbacks and frustrations.

Sharing in the lives of those kids you love so much is one of the true joys of marriage.

So talk about what you really want to talk about. Talk in the bleachers, in the car, over dinner, during a walk around the block, or getting ready for bed. When Mom and Dad connect in conversation about the kids, everyone wins.

— Question to Ask Out Loud —

Do we talk about the kids too much? (Alternately: Should we have kids? If so, when?)

"The value of marriage is not that adults produce children, but that children produce adults."

—Peter De Vries

25

Couples Need…

To Do unto Each Other

For husbands and wives everywhere, I unequivocally recommend Gary Chapman's book *The Five Love Languages*. He doesn't need my endorsement. I think that book and its spinoffs have sold a gazillion copies. Still, if you haven't read it, put down this book and grab that one. It'll change your perspective on relationships. Go ahead. I'll wait.

Are you back? So did you figure out your spouse's love language? Is it words of affirmation, quality time, receiving gifts, acts of service, or physical touch?

For the record, Mr. Chapman's book helped me quickly identify my bride's love language. It's receiving gifts. (Which reminds me that I need to do better in that area.) My love language is words of affirmation. (Rita does pretty well in this area.)

There are several strategies for uncovering your spouse's love language, and Chapman's book lays out a plan for any couple willing to put in the time. You could simply talk about it—but that seems like cheating. You could secretly and intentionally dedicate five extended seasons of your life to delivering each of the five different love languages and chart how your spouse responds. That seems daunting.

Perhaps the best way to figure out your spouse's love language is to pay careful attention to the things he or she does for you. There's a good chance that a wife who serves might like to be served. A husband who makes an extra effort to spend time with his wife might appreciate quality time. Touchers like to be touched. Encouragers like to be encouraged. Simply put, people sometimes give what they want to get.

And that's the point of this chapter. Which is about to get just a little steamy.

If one of the reasons you picked up this book is to revitalize your sex life, the answer may be easier to discern than you think. You might not have to buy anything, go anywhere, read a manual, change the sheets, or even light a scented candle.

Just consider for a moment how your husband or wife makes love to you. (Or attempts to make love to you.) Is there a touch here or a whisper there? Do they get romantic at a certain time of day? Or after certain events? Are there strokes and kisses that he initiates that she might not? Are there positions or stimulations she might set in motion, but he would almost never do on his own? Well, there's your answer.

Without deliberation or fanfare, go ahead and do those things. Again, these are things your spouse might do, but you wouldn't typically initiate yourself. Does something come to mind? Some idea or approach that has never been in your bag of tricks? If nothing hits you right away, it may require a bit more thought and a little more awareness on your part.

Don't agonize over this. Don't go beyond your comfort level. But also don't talk about it. That might spoil the mood or opportunity. It also might spoil a nice surprise. Instead, just do it and see where it leads.

Still not sure about the next steps? Let me get a little more specific.

Statistically, husbands initiate sex way more often than wives. It might even be a ratio of ten to one. So here's one idea for nine out of ten wives reading this: Prepare your heart and mind for a little romance and then let him know with a signal that isn't subtle at all. Your husband will be more than surprised and more than ready.

Conventional wisdom suggests that wives are more likely to slow things down in the early stages of a romantic encounter. So guys, take that cue. Instead of racing around to home plate, linger at first and second. You get the idea.

That's about as graphic as I'm going to get in this book. And so that's where we'll end this chapter. Except to add an apology for the chapter title. It's an obvious reference to Luke 6:31, "Do to others as you would have them do to you." Taken in context, I don't think Jesus was talking about marriage. The Golden Rule, as it's known, is usually applied to our relationship with our enemies. Still…it's something to think about.

— Question to Ask Out Loud —

Is there anything you've been hinting at for years that I've been totally missing—in the kitchen, around the house, in the car, or in our bedroom?

"There are two ways of spreading light:
to be the candle or the mirror that reflects it."

—EDITH WHARTON

Couples Need...

To Pull the Trigger

alfway through this book, you're getting the sense that most of
the strategies for strengthening your relationship are kept just
between the two of you. Quietly resolving to meet each other's needs.
Addressing bad habits. Taking a biblical view on marriage. Planning
fun little getaways and activities. Better communication. Better sex.
Learning to laugh more. And recommitting for the long haul.

This is life-changing stuff, but from the outside looking in, it doesn't
look like anything drastic or dramatic. Well, this chapter is about going
big. We're talking about the two of you making a big, public decision
to maybe even change the course of your life.

Some of these take cash, courage, and cooperation with others.
Looking at this list, you may think you're too old, too young, too broke,
or too set in your ways. That's nonsense.

Short-term mission trip. This is a no-brainer. Do this. Together. With
your church or with your favorite ministry, join with a team going
someplace to do real work with other believers. Make sure the trip is
at least ten days. And make sure it's not just a vacation and tour, but
includes hands-on ministry.

Full-time mission work. This is a much bigger decision. And may
take years of planning. God has to plant this seed in both your hearts.
If he does, nurture that idea and see where it takes you.

Lose 100 pounds (collectively). Most of us carry a few extra pounds.
What if you started eating better and working out together? Don't make
it an ultimatum. Or guilt trip. Make it a fun, daring, exhilarating quest.

Expect one of you to do much better than the other. Maybe start with an initial goal of 50 pounds, and if it's a 40/10 split, everyone still wins.

Have a baby. Or have another baby. Or adopt. Good, honest, intelligent, hardworking folks like you tend to raise good, honest, intelligent, hardworking kids. Frankly, the world needs more people like that. Don't worry about money. You'll figure out a way to feed them, buy school supplies, and send them to college. The love in your family will not be divided—it will be multiplied. Besides, you need someone to care for you in your old age, right? Plus, the more kids you have, the better chance you have of being blessed with a bunch of grandkids. "Children are a gift from the LORD; they are a reward from him" (Psalm 127:3 NLT).

Foster kids. Rita and I have welcomed ten foster babies into our home. My bride was driving that desire, but I totally got on board. I saw her heart and let her lead that decision. It serves as a great example of how husbands and wives should support each other as they identify and follow a calling. Being foster parents has been a blast. Besides, what could possibly be more important than taking in kids who need love?

Move. There are plenty of reasons to stay put. But there are also reasons to start fresh. Imagine a new neighborhood. A new town. A new state or province. Moving from rural to urban. Or vice versa. What would a dramatic move do to your relationship with each other? Or your relationship with others—family, friends, God?

Downsize your house. This could be very empowering. Suddenly your mortgage payment can be cut in half. And your life is no longer overwhelmed by paying bills on a tight budget. If you're not homeowners, maybe you can find a location where your living expenses are cut in half.

Run for office. Just after her fiftieth birthday, Rita was elected to the Saint Charles City Council. It's been a very cool experience for both of us. She's making a difference, and the two of us are suddenly having long, serious, fascinating, and surprising conversations on a wide range of issues. Your city, county, school board, and so on would all benefit from your thoughtful, biblical perspective.

Go back to school. Part-time. Full-time. Get your degree. Get your PhD. Maybe go to seminary. Put it this way: Two, three, or four years from now you will be two, three, or four years older. At that time, you will have that sheepskin or not. The choice is yours.

Leave the rat race. I'm not sure what this means. It could be different for every couple. But if you've been feeling like a rodent on a treadmill for more than a few years, please tell your spouse. Sometimes we do need to keep plodding along for a season of life. That's called being an adult. But you want to make sure that when you eventually cross the finish line, it's the right one.

Marriage retreat. Attending a weekend marriage conference may not be as flashy as the ten ideas above. But it can be equally as life changing. A story: My mom had a radical double mastectomy when she was 46 years old. My parents' solid marriage seemed to sail through that adversity without a bump. Later, I learned that my dad went several years before he had the courage to look at the disfiguring scars that often resulted with this aggressive surgery in the early 1970s. At a marriage retreat, Mom finally found the words to say, "Kenny, I need you to see." That weekend brought them closer than ever, and my parents would finish strong with 60 years of marriage. An organized conference focusing on your marriage might set the stage for your own diamond anniversary.

Anything else. Is there something on *your* list that didn't make *this* list? Something churning in the heart of him or her? Something that has bubbled up a bunch of times but keeps getting pushed back down because of circumstance, budget, fear, or common sense? Now is the time to reveal it to your beloved.

So? Is your soul stirred?

Dear husbands and wives, don't do any of these things next week. They're big deals and need to be carefully considered. But maybe the two of you should begin a dialogue on one or more of the above considerations. A little conversation. A little prayer. A little wise counsel from trusted mentors. Then maybe just do it. Pull the trigger.

Don't be surprised if you totally blow the minds of your neighbors, coworkers, pastors, friends, and family members. But you won't surprise God. He knew you had it in you the whole time.

— Question to Ask Out Loud —

Is it time to shake things up? If not now, when?

"Trust in the LORD with all your heart
and lean not on your own understanding;
in all your ways submit to him,
and he will make your paths straight."

—PROVERBS 3:5-6

27

Couples Need…

To Save Up for a Second Honeymoon

G ary and Sherry (not their real names) have a giant pickle jar filled with Hamiltons, Jacksons, Grants, and even a few Benjamins. They've been saving up for a second honeymoon that hasn't officially happened yet.

They began putting money in a smaller jar just after their first anniversary more than 20 years ago. As young marrieds, they couldn't afford to go anywhere special, so they agreed to start socking money away until they could go on their dream vacation.

The destination for their dream second honeymoon has changed over the years. From Paris to Bora-Bora to Australia to maybe even buying a vacation home on a lake up north. The jar has also changed over the years. From a regular-size mayonnaise jar to an antique one-gallon pickle jar they found at a flea market. Every couple of years, the contents of the jar are dumped out on their bed, counted, and transferred to a high-yield savings account, which they still call "the pickle jar." As in, "Hey, how much is in the pickle jar?"

Saving for a second honeymoon is a really, really, really good idea. But the real story is how, when, and why Gary and Sherry add money to the pickle jar.

It started as a tease. Which became a dare. Which blossomed into an inside joke and secret code just between the two of them. (Which is why I can't use their real names.)

Every time they have sex, one of them has to put in a ten spot. If either of them asks for special favors or maneuvers, it might cost twenty.

If they both climax at the same time, they need to somehow come up with a fifty-dollar bill to put in the jar. And if they do something really naughty or slightly illegal, one of them will be unscrewing that jar and putting in a hundred dollar bill. Gary and Sherry wouldn't go into any more specifics, and that's probably a good thing.

You can imagine some of the charming and provocative conversations that have taken place over the years.

"Can I borrow twenty bucks?" "Oh, what for?"

"It looks like we're getting a tax refund of $1200. I wonder what I can get with that?"

"We could spend $60 on dinner out or order a $20 pizza and invest the $40 in the pickle jar."

"Look what I found in this pair of blue jeans! A folded-up fifty!"

"There's a sale on dishwashers at Home Depot. $100 off! What do you think?"

Dozens of times in the last two decades, Gary has wordlessly pulled a ten-dollar bill out of his wallet and slid it across the table to his bride. He says it works about two-thirds of the time. That's not a bad average. Sometimes Sherry might take the bill and say, "Let's call that a deposit for Friday night." Of course, that's a perfectly acceptable response.

What will Gary and Sherry do with the thousands of dollars they have accumulated? Really, it doesn't matter. They could put that tidy sum toward a trip for two, a vacation home, a remodeling project, college for their kids, retirement, or simply an emergency fund. In my mind, Gary and Sherry have already figured out a way to invest in a honeymoon that never ends.

— Question to Ask Out Loud —

Sweetheart, what should we save up for?

"Saving love doesn't bring any interest."

—Mae West

28

Couples Need…

To Think Twice About Going Solo to the Kennedy Space Center

I'm confident that the other 51 chapters in this book are accurate, valuable, insightful, and brilliant. But I'm not sure about the following advice. Read it, mull over it, talk about it with your spouse, and let me know what you think.

I'm recalling a TV commercial shoot I did in Vero Beach, Florida, more than 20 years ago. Working for the Campbell Mithun agency in Chicago, I had written a spot for the Kroger supermarket chain. The 30-second commercial promoting their wide selection of items featured the image of a stock boy leaping off a pyramid of cartons and not-so-clever dialogue, like "There's more in store at Kroger."

The unmarried agency producer, the unmarried art director, and this married copywriter flew down to sunny Florida for an entire week. It was a routine trip for an advertising professional, but it left my young wife and three sons to endure several winter days without me. Why did we need a week? We did casting on Monday, location meetings on Tuesday, and filming Wednesday night. Thursday was set aside for film processing, and Friday we reviewed the footage before flying home. We couldn't leave town until we knew the video and audio were usable. Which meant all three of us from the agency had nothing to do on Thursday. The veteran producer announced he would be taking the rental car and making the hour-long trip up the coast to tour the John F. Kennedy Space Center at Cape Canaveral. He invited me along.

What a cool opportunity. I love taking side trips to explore places that exist nowhere else. As a child of the space age, I had watched many hours of live television coverage of the Gemini and Apollo missions. This was my first time to the Florida coast, I didn't know when I might return, and the decision was a no-brainer…I simply couldn't go.

My thought process went something like this. *With my wife and boys stuck at home, I don't have the right to such a wonderful adventure. How could I go home—even with a suitcase of souvenirs—and tell them about seeing rockets and space suits and moon rocks? My first trip to the JFK Space Center will have to be with my family.*

That was the decision I made. And I'm not sure it was the right one. The motivation was healthy. I would have felt a little guilty, but mostly I know that I would have spent the entire tour regretting that my family was not with me. The two-part punchline is that Rita later told me, "You should have gone!" and two decades later I've still never made it to Cape Canaveral with or without my family.

What does this have to do with connecting as a couple? Just as there were two sides to my long-ago decision, there are two sides to similar decisions you will make. When either of you has a chance to do something spontaneous on your own, you should have the freedom to do so. Still, your grandest life memories should be made with your spouse (or your family). That includes planned vacations, sightseeing adventures, major sporting events, exploring national landmarks, and most once-in-a-lifetime opportunities.

Shared experiences and memories unify husbands and wives. Your day-to-day care, provision, and sacrifices establish the firm foundation of a marriage. But the outstanding adventures of life bookmark the passage of time. Extraordinary places and events etch permanent images in your memory bank. If those images belong only to him or her, they can't really be shared. Those memories may even be divisive.

Can a husband head off with three best buddies for a fly-in fishing trip to northern Canada? Sure. Can a wife and three gal pals spend a long weekend in Manhattan, shopping and seeing a couple Broadway shows? Absolutely. It all sounds like fun.

But be careful. If your sweetest or most dramatic memories in the *past* 12 months are not with your spouse, then make some intentional changes in the *next* 12 months.

So. My recommendation—and I could be wrong—is to say no to most invitations to social events and outings that don't include your spouse. Does that sound overly cautious? Am I implying that spouses can't be trusted on their own for a few hours or a few days? Is this author being a spoilsport, taking the enjoyment out of life? That's not my intent. Allow me to remove the double negative from the above recommendation. Seek out and say *yes* to social events and outings that *do* include your spouse.

Back to the business trip conundrum. One of the great goals in life is to find a career and work alongside colleagues that bring meaning and satisfaction to that part of your life. But out-of-town trade shows, conventions, sales calls, and commercial productions should be mostly business. Put still another way, walking in your front door and reuniting with your family should be the best part of the trip.

— Question to Ask Out Loud —

How would you feel if I was out of town on business and I did something by myself or with a colleague that you and I would typically enjoy doing together?

"When you live with another person for 50 years, all of your memories are invested in that person, like a bank account of shared memories. It's not that you refer to them constantly. In fact, for people who do not live in the past, you almost never say, 'Do you remember that night we…?' But you don't have to. That is the best of

all. You know that the other person does remember. Thus, the past is part of the present as long as the other person lives. It is better than any scrapbook, because you are both living scrapbooks."

—FEDERICO FELLINI

29

Couples Need...

To Leave Notes

One of my business cards is tucked into a corner of the mirror above Rita's dresser in our bedroom. The printed side is facing the glass. On the back are the words. "Love you. XXXO." It's been there five years.

As I was packing to leave on a three-day business trip, it took me about 20 seconds to pull out that card, flip it over, print two words and four letters, and put it on her pillow, where she would find it later that evening. That miniscule action is still paying dividends five years later.

For the record, three X's and one O is my go-to signature for just about all the correspondence I do with Rita, including notes, emails, greeting cards, and even texts. Where did that come from? I'm glad you asked.

Each time I type or write "XXXO," the same vocal cadence goes through my head in the voice of—believe it or not—Mel Brooks: "Kisses, kisses, kisses. Hug!"

You probably don't remember the commercial, but it's one of my favorites. And it may have been one of the reasons I got into advertising back in the day. The 1973 spot opens with a grandma wearing a housedress, sitting at an old kitchen table, attempting to write a letter with various kinds of fruit. Here's the entire voiceover script.

> MEL BROOKS: Don't write with a peach. If you write with a peach, you'll get a very wet letter. Don't write with a prune. Words will come out wrinkled and dopey. Let's face it. The only fruit you can write with is a banana. The

Bic Banana. A fine line marker. Not to be confused with a ballpoint.

Writing a letter to your son, write right. Usually you write, "Dear Son, how are you? I'm fine." Write that same letter with a Bic Banana, and you get, "Dear Sonny, I miss your face! Mom." See what a nice letter it writes. Kisses. Kisses. Kisses.

And it comes in colors. Most fruits only come in one color, except grapes, which come in two colors and, of course, pits and pitless.

Look, if you've got to write with a fruit, write with a Bic Banana. It's only 29 cents. Your best buy in writing fruit. Kisses. Kisses. Kisses. Hug. The Bic Banana. A different way to write.

It's not romantic, but it's hilarious. To me, anyway. And thanks for letting me share. On YouTube, search for "Bic Banana 1973" and watch it yourself.

Anyway. Here's the point. When you leave town, leave a note. Be creative. Be silly. Be romantic. Be short. Be nice. And don't forget to include lots of *X*'s and *O*'s.

My old college friend Larry gets this idea. He wrote, "When either of us needs to be away overnight for work, we leave each other notes and messages in unexpected places—stuck in a toothbrush, tucked inside the pillowcase, taped to the bottle of milk in the refrigerator."

Of course, a few days apart may not seem like a big deal anymore. Emails, texts, and video chat all seem to make absence less of an issue. But being there is not the same as being here. And being remembered and appreciated with little notes still brings warm fuzzies. That's why that business card is still tucked into the corner of our bedroom mirror.

Oh yeah. When you write those notes, please use a pen or pencil. As Mel Brooks so clearly stated. "If you write with a peach, you'll get a very wet letter. Don't write with a prune. Words will come out wrinkled and dopey."

— Question to Ask Out Loud —

What can I do to make sure you aren't lonely when I head out of town for a few days?

"This is not a letter,
but my arms around you for a brief moment."

—Katherine Mansfield

30

Couples Need…

To Cherish Anniversaries

You've probably seen the year-by-year list of anniversary gifts based on traditional or modern customs. The PR departments of retailers like Hallmark and Macy's might publicize the list to encourage store traffic and creative gift giving. Pinterest and women's magazines get some mileage out of the list on a regular basis. I don't know any couples who have steadfastly exchanged annual gifts based on this chart, but let's review it anyway.

It's a good excuse to recall your nuptials and consider how the seasons of life unfold. From paper to cotton to wood to iron. Getting stronger and more precious each year.

Anniversary	Traditional	Modern
1	paper	clocks
2	cotton	china
3	leather	crystal/glass
4	linen/silk	appliances
5	wood	silverware
6	iron	wood
7	wool/copper	desk sets

8	bronze	linens/lace
9	pottery	leather
10	tin/aluminum	diamond jewelry
15	crystal	watches
20	china	platinum
25	silver	silver
30	pearl	diamond
35	coral	jade
40	ruby	ruby
45	sapphire	sapphire
50	gold	gold
55	emerald	emerald
60	diamond	diamond
65	blue sapphire	blue sapphire
70	platinum	platinum

With life expectancies increasing, it's quite possible that you could go for the gold. If you're just settling in to your first decade, it may seem like a long way off. But ask any couple celebrating with rubies or sapphires, and they'll tell you it goes by quickly. Most will also affirm that except for a few healthy bumps along the way, it gets better and better.

The topic of anniversary gifts leads me to ask these two questions, which could be quite eye-opening to some couples: Do you think husbands and wives typically exchange presents on their anniversary? Or does only the husband buy presents?

Guys and gals, did your answers match?

That might sound like a silly question because everyone knows spouses both buy for each other, right? Not so fast. In some families, apparently, tradition dictates that anniversary gift giving is one-way—husband to wife. Coming into our marriage, that was Rita's understanding. But that concept took me totally by surprise. What's really funny is that Rita and I didn't realize our different viewpoints until we had been married almost ten years.

Think about that for a second. Put yourself in my shoes. For our first nine anniversaries, I listened for hints, checked the budget, shopped and wrapped in secret, and presented her with a more-or-less thoughtful gift. What did I get in return? Pretty much just a card, a kiss, and a thank-you. That's really okay. After all, cash was tight, and my needs have always been simple.

Looking back, gift receiving during that decade was marked by some mild confusion and a twinge of annual disappointment. Rita had always been generous on Christmas, birthdays, and Valentine's Day. During the year, she'd even buy or make me a gift for no reason at all. But in my mind, she didn't feel the need to honor the day we were married.

I was never ticked off about this seemingly unfair imbalance of gift giving, and it was never something we talked about. Finally, in a casual conversation, some married friends were talking about exchanging anniversary gifts, and Rita was genuinely surprised that *she* bought a gift for *him*. That's when it all came clear. Our family traditions were different.

We laughed about it. We debated the issue, and the gift giving has since pretty much balanced out. That makes me glad, and it also makes me wonder how many other couples are experiencing the same misunderstanding.

So here are the takeaways from this chapter: (1) Be thoughtful about anniversary gifts, (2) go for the gold, and (3) determine if she has some ground to make up because she hasn't been buying gifts for the last X number of years.

— Question to Ask Out Loud —

What would you like for our next anniversary?

"A wedding anniversary is the celebration of love, trust, partnership, tolerance and tenacity. The order varies for any given year."

—Paul Sweeney

31

Couples Need...

To Split Vacations

No, I'm not recommending couples take separate vacations. The simple point of this chapter is to make sure the time and money you invest in your vacation generates an experience that feels like a vacation for both of you.

For Rita and me, sometimes that's not so easy. She's a relaxer. I'm an explorer.

If we're at a seaside resort, Rita is perfectly content to read a book on the beach. If we're in a big city, she would be perfectly happy strolling the sights within a few blocks of the hotel. If we're going to an obvious mecca of tourism, there's no reason to do a lot of planning and scheduling. Head for the top attractions and return to the hotel room *before* your feet hurt. In our nation's capital, head for the monuments. In Orlando, do Disney. In Door County, the best plan is clearly just to walk the Main Street shops and go to a fish boil.

Rita's philosophy is to let the destination reveal itself naturally. In other words, *a vacation should be a vacation.* Conversely, I think a vacation is a chance to do, do, and do things you don't normally do. That takes advance scheduling and plenty of colorful brochures and website printouts. Our different approach to travel is more proof that successful marriages are built on overlapping and intertwining gifts and preferences.

If that sounds at all like your relationship, then take extra care when you start choosing destinations and planning itineraries. Let's face it—mountain climbers don't always marry other mountain climbers. Opera lovers don't always marry other opera lovers. Relaxers sometimes marry explorers. You can't possibly please both of you. Or can you?

The answer to this dilemma is not rocket science: During your time away, stick together and make sure you do some of her stuff, some of his stuff, and some mutual stuff.

You could make the case that it would be perfectly acceptable for Jay to go deep-sea fishing while Rita reads on her beach blanket. If that uses just one day out of seven, that's probably a good plan. Over dinner that evening I would tell her about the marlin that got away, and she would describe the amusing mass of humanity strolling the shoreline that day. That single day of solo activities would not consume our entire vacation and would probably even add some interest.

However, if you've been paying attention, this book and this author endorse time together as a unifying factor. If that means one of you leaves your comfort zone, that's a plus! Your spouse should receive it as a gift. It's not a sacrifice—it's an investment.

That doesn't mean forcing your beloved to do stuff they hate or physically can't do. No one wants a seasick vacation partner. If your spouse is claustrophobic, don't go spelunking. If your spouse is acrophobic, don't go parasailing. After seeing Rita's allergic reaction during a trail ride in Estes Park, Colorado, I will never suggest we go horseback riding again.

But I don't regret going to that quilt show she dragged me to. And Rita really did enjoy the roller coaster rides I "made" her take with me. Thankfully, we are on the same page for most vacations and long weekends. Some knickknack browsing. Some museum exploring. Some trail hiking. Some bleacher sitting. Some café chatting. Which still leaves time for me to do what she wants and her to do what I want.

Like I said—her stuff, his stuff, mutual stuff. It isn't rocket science.

— Question to Ask Out Loud —

What's your dream vacation? Why haven't we taken it?

"We hit the sunny beaches where we occupy ourselves keeping the sun off our skin, the saltwater off our bodies, and the sand out of our belongings."

—ERMA BOMBECK

32

Couples Need…

To Acknowledge Sex
as a Spiritual Act

Let's read a few of the steamier passages from Song of Songs.

> You are altogether beautiful, my darling;
>> there is no flaw in you (4:7).
> My beloved is radiant and ruddy,
>> outstanding among ten thousand (5:10).
> Come away, my beloved,
>> and be like a gazelle
> or like a young stag
>> on the spice-laden mountains (8:14).
> Let him kiss me with the kisses of his mouth—
>> for your love is more delightful than wine (1:2).
> Your cheeks are beautiful with earrings,
>> your neck with strings of jewels (1:10).
> I am a wall,
>> and my breasts are like towers.
> Thus I have become in his eyes
>> like one bringing contentment (8:10).
> Your breasts are like two fawns,
>> like twin fawns of a gazelle
>> that browse among the lilies (4:5).
> Take me away with you—let us hurry!
>> Let the king bring me into his chambers.

We rejoice and delight in you;
  we will praise your love more than wine.
How right they are to adore you! (1:4).
Let us go early to the vineyards
  to see if the vines have budded,
if their blossoms have opened,
  and if the pomegranates are in bloom—
  there I will give you my love (7:12).
His left arm is under my head,
  and his right arm embraces me (2:6).
I said, "I will climb the palm tree;
  I will take hold of its fruit."
May your breasts be like clusters of grapes on the vine,
  the fragrance of your breath like apples (7:8).
Your navel is a rounded goblet
  that never lacks blended wine.
Your waist is a mound of wheat
  encircled by lilies (7:2).
I belong to my beloved,
  and his desire is for me.
Come, my beloved, let us go to the countryside,
  let us spend the night in the villages (7:10-11).
Many waters cannot quench love;
  rivers cannot sweep it away.
If one were to give
  all the wealth of one's house for love,
  it would be utterly scorned (8:7).
My beloved has gone down to his garden,
  to the beds of spices,
to browse in the gardens
  and to gather lilies.
I am my beloved's and my beloved is mine;
  he browses among the lilies (6:2-3).

> Your breasts are like two fawns,
> > like twin fawns of a gazelle (7:3).
> Like an apple tree among the trees of the forest
> > is my beloved among the young men.
> I delight to sit in his shade,
> > and his fruit is sweet to my taste.
> Let him lead me to the banquet hall,
> > and let his banner over me be love (2:3-4).

I make no claims to be a biblical scholar. But I believe there are several clear recommendations in these passages for married couples. That includes going to the countryside and staying at a nice bed-and-breakfast. Kissing. Saying nice things about each other. Buying jewelry. Thinking about sex and talking about it. Offering obvious invitations for romance.

Perhaps the most beguiling attribute of Song of Songs (also called Song of Solomon) is the mystery surrounding the choice of suggestive words and imagery. No body parts or sexual acts are mentioned, which means graphic-sounding passages should be interpreted with care. Respected pastor and Bible scholar John MacArthur says it well.

> Since the symbolism [in Song of Songs] is obviously about passion, romance, love, desire, and tenderness, its ambiguity serves a deliberate purpose: it speaks in secret terms about that which should be kept secret. The language is clearly designed to communicate intimate affection privately through veiled, confidential, almost clandestine terms.
>
> This is a vital point: The style of communication between these two lovers beautifully conceals all but the most essential meaning of their love songs in a way that guards the deeply personal (and divinely intended) privacy of the marriage bed.
>
> Song of Solomon is incredibly beautiful precisely because it is so carefully veiled. It is a perfect description

of the wonderful, tender, intimate discovery that God designed to take place between a young man and his bride in a place of secrecy. We are not told in vivid terms what all the metaphors mean, because the beauty of marital passion is in the eye of the beholder—where it should stay.[13]

Frankly, I'm glad that a relatively small number of unmarried individuals will be reading this chapter. Song of Songs should really be read and interpreted from the perspective of a man and woman in a loving, monogamous marriage relationship. It's clearly meant to conjure up images and even fantasies, the object of which should be your husband or wife.

Finally, if you'll allow me a personal interpretation. Song of Songs suggests a very distinct sense of transferred ownership created by marriage. "I am my beloved's and my beloved is mine" (6:3). It proposes that husbands and wives give their entire selves as a gift to their beloved. We hold nothing back. We trust. We surrender. We open with care. We give thanks. I believe that's the goal.

— Question to Ask Out Loud —

Do you feel like we have surrendered to each other?

"When a man and a woman give themselves to each other in an act of marital love, they can know the love of Christ as no one else can know it."

—J. Vernon McGee

33

Couples Need...

To Cry and Laugh Together

It would be logical to assume most of your major arguments happen when you are both having bad days. Frustrations and disappointments simmer for hours and finally explode when you are in each other's company. You've both trained yourselves not to throw tantrums at work, in public, at church, with the kids, or in front of the neighbors. But when it's just the two of you, you feel as if you can finally just let it out. (I'm not sure whether that's a good thing or bad thing.) "We were both having a bad day" is also a convenient excuse for irascible behavior.

But I submit the biggest husband-wife arguments, the ones that leave the deepest scars, occur when one of you is having a terrible, horrible, no good, very bad day, and the other is having just the opposite.

Here's how that situation might unfold. All week he's looking forward to Saturday, when he gets to do his thing—fishing, golf, hunting, Civil War reenactment, a car show, softball, tailgating at his alma maters' football game, whatever. As he heads out the door, his bride even wishes him well because she knows he'll have fun, and besides, she's got plans for her own rewarding and relaxing day.

Unfortunately, every part of the day she imagines crumbles or backfires. She can't find her good jeans, and the top she wanted to wear has an unidentified green stain on the sleeve. The friend she was supposed to meet at Panera cancels because of a sick kid. A clerk is rude, gas has gone up 22 cents, the trick for fixing her iPhone glitch that always works doesn't work this time, and the amazing craft store worth the 45-minute drive from home has gone out of business. Which she discovers in the store parking lot.

Great day for him. Not so for her. The couple—who very much love each other—pull in the driveway at the same time. He has a big smile on his face and…that's the last straw. Whatever he says or doesn't say, whatever he does or doesn't do, will cause her to bite his head off. "You idiot, you parked on the hose!" "You lazy slob, you didn't weed-whack along the fence." "You inconsiderate jerk, you drove off with my sunglasses in your car."

It works the other way around too. It's just an average weekday, but for some reason her hair looks great. Last week's manicure is still pristine. It's a skinny day. She dominates in two meetings and personally closes the deal with a new client, thereby preventing multiple layoffs next quarter. She feels empowered and worthy for the first time in a long time. It's an A-plus day. Much to the contrary, his ego has spent the last ten hours being dragged through the mud. At home, he spends the evening growling, cursing, and brooding, interrupted by bursts of self-pity.

Wouldn't it be wonderful if the spouse experiencing a good day could elevate the spouse experiencing the bad day? It typically doesn't work that way. Instead, Mr. Grouchy or Mrs. Frustrated goes on the attack, intentionally accusing the other party of a lack of understanding or compassion. No one really communicates. Sniping remarks whiz back and forth between the dueling couple. When the volume finally dies down, he and she are both left wondering if they married the wrong person.

As Christians, our true circumstance doesn't really change, even during the highs and lows of daily life. We can and should be able to focus on the eternal joy we have in Christ. Starting each day with that reminder will go a long way toward eliminating all terrible, horrible days in general. Unfortunately, we forget, we take our eyes off Jesus, and our sinful nature sometimes blinds us to his promise.

If you find yourself in the midst of a torrential convergence of highs and lows, consider the clear instructions in one of my favorite Bible verses. It's Romans 12:15. Read it and then say it out loud. "Rejoice with those who rejoice; mourn with those who mourn." It doesn't matter who is smart enough to put this advice into action. The idea is to make a conscious choice to match your spouse's emotions whether they're high or low.

You really do love and care about each other, so if one of you is having a cruddy day, the other should quickly pick up on those signals and literally share in their grief. "Sweetheart, I'm so sorry," or "Pookie, come get a hug from your Cuddle Bunny," are much nicer things to say than "You had a bad day! I get it! But don't drag me down with you."

If one of you had a tremendous day but the other is still steaming, it would be nice if the spouse who happens to be on top of the world would jump down and mourn right alongside their hurting beloved. But it's also possible—and even preferable—for the person in the pits to leave a smidge of room for the Holy Spirit to work. Our first human instinct when we hit bottom is to feel sorry for ourselves. But the courageous Christian will take a step back, evaluate the situation, and look at the big picture. If we see our spouse standing in the sunshine, we can choose to follow the instructions of Romans 12 and join them in their joy.

In any case, the goal is to mourn together or rejoice together. What shouldn't happen is that you take your Top Ten Day and your spouse's Zero Day and average them out. Living with mediocre days is no fun at all. Personally, I would much rather cry with Rita or laugh with Rita than just exist in denial of our emotions.[14]

— Question to Ask Out Loud —

Which one of us is more likely to try to cheer the other one up? How often does it work? How often do we share each other's pain? What happens when we do?

"May the God of hope fill you with all joy and peace as you trust in him, so that you may overflow with hope by the power of the Holy Spirit."

—Romans 15:13

34

Couples Need…

To Do a 180 on Those Bad Habits

One of the most challenging habits to break for young wrestlers is "locked hands." If you're a former wrestler or coach, you know exactly what I'm talking about. In high school and youth wrestling, when a boy is "on top," his primary goal is to turn his opponent on his back for a pin. Sometimes, though, the wrestler on top finds himself hanging on for dear life, simply trying not to lose his advantage by getting "reversed" or allowing his opponent to "escape." One strategy is to wrap your arm around the other guy's waist and grab your own hand or wrist. Except that's illegal. That's "locked hands" and results in a penalty point.

Teaching beginning wrestlers not to lock hands is one of the great frustrations for a coach. From the edge of the mat, you can shout, "Don't lock your hands," but the wrestler just can't help it. Locking hands is instinctive. As soon as those two hands touch, the ref blows the whistle, stops the match, and awards a penalty point. That's why a smart coach doesn't even bother yelling, "Don't lock your hands." Instead, he gives a proactive command for the wrestler to do something else with his hands. By calling out, "deep waist," "pick an ankle," "break him down," or "grab a wrist," the wrestler is given something to do besides just hang on. Plus, it may lead to something even better—turning your opponent on his back.

By suggesting something proactive, you prevent the penalty and advance your cause. You're replacing a negative with a positive. That strategy works in real life too:

- Want to stop smoking? Don't just say no to nicotine—say yes to celery.

- Want to cut down on desserts? Take a walk after dinner.

- Want to stop yelling at referees? Volunteer to keep score, shoot game video, work the concession stand, work the chain gang, or be the ref.

- Want to watch less TV? Make a regular weekly trip to the library.

How about a few applications for your marriage? Men...

- Instead of walking away from a sink sprinkled in whiskers, take an extra 37 seconds and wipe down the entire counter and maybe even grab the Windex and wipe those water spots off your bathroom mirror.

- Instead of forgetting your anniversary on June 17, celebrate on the seventeenth of every month.

- Instead of jam-packing too many activities into your travel plans, schedule one or two days of your vacation as do-nothing days.

- Instead of buying a Valentine's Day gift at the last minute, order something online as soon as the calendar turns to February. (It's so less stressful.)

- Instead of trying to guilt your bride into sex tonight, ask her out on a romantic date for the upcoming weekend and make all the arrangements.

- Instead of giving her gifts that look like they were wrapped by a chimp, have them gift wrapped at the store.

Women...

- Instead of nagging him to replace or repair the what-chamacallit, thank him for what he has already done around your home.

- Instead of trashing your husband to your girlfriends, choose to regularly say something wonderful about him. (Would you rather have them feel sorry for you or be just a little envious?)

- Instead of withholding sex as a punishment, initiate sex as a way to get closer to your husband. (That's how God designed it!)

- Instead of buying another pair of shoes and hiding the receipt, donate three rarely worn pairs to Goodwill.

- Instead of sending him indiscernible signals and hoping he reads your mind, just tell him what you want. (He really does want to meet your every desire.)

Both of you...

- Instead of stomping out of the room and slamming the door after an argument, stop yourself, turn around, and say, "I'm sorry. I feel terrible when we argue."

- Instead of assessing blame, take responsibility.

- Instead of comparing your spouse to old boyfriends and girlfriends, look to the future with hope and optimism.

- Instead of always needing to win the argument, do what it takes to win the relationship. (Even if you're right!)

- Instead of rolling your eyes at the silly suggestions in this book, consider the underlying truth.

The idea of replacing negative personal habits with positive habits can work in all kinds of situations—on the job, with kids, in many personal interactions. Go ahead and try it. But since this is a book for couples, you are encouraged to start right there.

— Question to Ask Out Loud —

What two or three relational bad habits could I replace with positive habits?

"The mind governed by the flesh is hostile to God; it does not submit to God's law, nor can it do so."

—ROMANS 8:7

35

Couples Need…

To Insist on the Real Thing

This chapter is a warning about fake jewelry. And fake love.

I almost got scammed twice. By the same jewelry store. You would think I would be smarter than that. Here's the slightly amusing, cautionary tale.

Rita somehow got me to agree to buy her a new bracelet for each grandkid that comes along. Not a platinum and diamond tennis bracelet that breaks the bank. Merely something her girlfriends will appreciate and something worth passing on years from now for granddaughters to wear and grandsons to give to their future wives. As of this writing, Rita is jangling three bracelets for Jackson, Judah, and Emerson.

Shopping for bracelet number two, I found this really interesting piece at a reputable local jewelry store. It featured a band of striking dark gray cut stones—luminous but not translucent—and I was told it was "marcasite." The price seemed fair, so I brought it home. Rita loved it. And a couple days later I did some simple online research.

What I discovered was marcasite is another name for iron pyrite, which is another name for fool's gold. That's right. The sales clerk had taken me, quite literally, for a fool. I wanted to march back down to the store and make a small scene, but Rita really did like the piece (so did I), and it made for a fun story. So one of Rita's favorite pieces right now is a bracelet featuring angle-cut fool's gold.

Surprisingly, the quest for bracelet number three took me to the same store. As the only customer in the store, I joked with all three of the staff about my purchase from a year earlier. It was all very friendly. On the same display rack was another reasonably priced bracelet that caught my eye. The stones featured were described as cultured diamonds, and they looked good to me. So I said, "Wrap it up." While they were processing my order, I heard one of the women behind the counter say "zirconia." And I said, "Wait. This is cubic zirconia?" With their reply, I breathed out slowly, thanked them for their time, and headed for the exit. Apparently, the term "cultured diamond" is the latest euphemism for a man-made diamond. Consider yourself warned.

Needless to say, we found a bracelet celebrating Emerson's birth at another jewelry store.

So here's the deal. I'm not a snob or a fashion guru. I understand cubic zirconia and marcasite are fun and sparkly and may even be considered stylish and in vogue. But in my old-school mind, it's fake jewelry. I'd much rather Rita wore a simple band or bracelet with no stones than one with man-made stones.

In the same way, I will not settle for fake love. And neither should you.

You can tell fake love because it's selfish. Or it's for show. Fake love is dating the prettiest girl only because she's the prettiest girl. Fake love is getting engaged only so you can plan a lavish reception. Fake love is being charming and gracious to your spouse at a social gathering but then being rude and bitter on the drive home. Fake love has conditions: "I'll love you if…" "I'll love you when…" "I'll love you until something better comes along."

Funny thing about fake love. With time, commitment, thoughtful appreciation, respect, and mutual submission, I believe fake love can become real. (Unlike jewelry.)

That's one of the reasons God is so adamant against divorce. He knows that many newlyweds aren't really in love. They may think they are, but they've got a long way to go. For some couples, the first real disagreement after the honeymoon takes them by surprise. The idea of the "seven-year itch" suggests that marriages start to fizzle once the husband and wife really know each other. Empty nesters sometimes split up because they can't see anything beyond their role as parents. But God—the designer of marriage—has provided everything couples need to go the distance.

The formula begins and ends with committing to the commitment. You can't possibly establish resilience and staying power in the first intoxicating days of wedded bliss. Great marriages take time. Divorce often kills love before it can take root.

To build (or strengthen) real love, husbands and wives need to dig deep when discussing important issues, making sure conversations are more than just superficial. You need to invest time and thought into your relationship. Not because you have to, but because you want to. Real love puts your spouse's needs before your own. Real love looks for the good. Real love keeps promises, forgives quickly, and defends the honor of your beloved. The Bible gives high priority to authentic love.

> If I speak in the tongues of men or of angels, but do not have love, I am only a resounding gong or a clanging cymbal. If I have the gift of prophecy and can fathom all mysteries and all knowledge, and if I have a faith that can move mountains, but do not have love, I am nothing. If I give all I possess to the poor and give over my body to hardship that I may boast, but do not have love, I gain nothing (1 Corinthians 13:1-3).

Don't settle for a marriage of fake love. Don't panic if you feel unlovable or unloving. Those are feelings, not facts. Keep looking for real love that has an undercurrent that keeps life and relationships moving forward. Couples experiencing real love share struggles, regrets, and disappointments without fear. Loving husbands and wives listen and respond with genuine care. And by the way, no one should be faking anything in the marriage bed either.

There is a difference between fake jewelry and fake love. When you buy marcasite or cultured diamonds, you can take them back. When a married couple senses a moment of fake love, they need to recommit to their vows and their future. And pray expectantly for God to honor his commitment to make them "one flesh."

— Question to Ask Out Loud —

Which would you rather receive—a huge cubic zirconia or a small, tasteful, authentic diamond?

"Generally, by the time you are Real, most of your hair has been loved off, and your eyes drop out and you get loose in the joints and very shabby. But these things don't matter at all, because once you are Real you can't be ugly, except to people who don't understand."

—Margery Williams, *The Velveteen Rabbit*

36

Couples Need...

To Pay Off Their Credit Cards

You won't be surprised to hear that experts say finance is the number two cause of marital discord. Money management issues hit couples at every income level. It doesn't matter how much money is coming in—there always seems to be a wee bit more going out.

All of us like to keep up with the Joneses. Some of us, unfortunately, need to keep *ahead* of the Joneses. It's a classic marital clash. Frugal versus prodigal. Saving for retirement versus enjoying life now. Buying a new car every year versus seeing if you can reach 200,000 on the odometer. Bloomingdales versus Walmart. First class versus coach. Paying big bucks for private pitching lessons for your son or daughter versus letting them play just for the fun of it. Tithing a full 10 percent versus putting ten bucks in the basket each week.

And unexpected expenses always seem to blow the budget (if there is a budget).

For many married couples, the arguments about money are loud and frequent. Sometimes—and maybe this is even worse—discord over financial priorities remains unspoken and hidden just below the surface.

After about nine years of marriage, such was the case with my friend and his wife. To outsiders, they looked comfortable and content. One nice house. Two nice cars. Three nice kids. But there was an unspoken unrest. The basic monthly bills were mostly getting paid. Income and outgo was just about even. But both wife and husband had a sense something was missing. Both were working full-time. He was also working on his MBA.

Looking back, the signs were clear. A bonus he had been counting on didn't come through. She was hiding purchases—not big things, but items that weren't necessities. Health insurance rates had notched up more than expected. Three or four household appliances had died in a short period of time. And most telling of all, their three credit cards were maxed out, and they were making minimum payments.

Both he and she knew something had to change. And things got quiet for a few days. A confrontation was brewing.

It's unclear who spoke first. Maybe—like on a TV sitcom—they both spoke at the same time. She said she wanted to turn life up a notch with a bigger house and fancier vacations, which would require more income. In the same instant, he blurted out an entire string of expenses that had to be slashed. Sell one of their cars. Downsize their home. Take the kids out of private school. Cancel vacation plans. And then he went on a ten-minute rant on how she spent "a thousand dollars every month at Starbucks."

They both knew something was wrong. They both knew it had something to do with cash flow. And they both overreacted. It turned out to be one of the best days of their married life because they finally started to talk.

Before that moment, she had not known what he was going through. He would try to sit down once a month to tackle bills, but that was impossible. He actually had to think about bills *every single day* because he paid them online at the last possible minute. It was endlessly exhausting. Plus, he hadn't told her about the bonus that never happened. He finally confessed that his pride had gotten in the way of admitting he couldn't give her everything she wanted.

In a miraculous turn of events, it turns out he *could* give her everything she wanted. To her great credit, this thirtysomething wife responded with sensitivity, wisdom, love, and trust. She came to realize all she really needed was rooted in relationship. And that can't be bought. In a stunningly short time, that entire family shifted their focus from looking inward to looking out.

A new story was being written. That day of reckoning, which could have driven them apart, had driven them together. They knew everything was going to be okay when they both laughed after realizing her Starbucks tab was more like 60 bucks per month. (Which is still a lot.)

They did cut back and paid off their credit cards within 18 months. Which led to a celebration much bigger than you may expect. Carrying a zero monthly balance is a worthy goal for every couple.

You also won't be surprised to hear that God—who had been relegated to an occasional guest in their home—was soon given ownership of all they had. And he gave back a hundredfold.

— Question to Ask Out Loud —

What's our outstanding credit card balance?

"Money never made a man happy yet, nor will it. The more a man has, the more he wants. Instead of filling a vacuum, it makes one."

—BENJAMIN FRANKLIN

37

Couples Need...

To Tell Their Story

This is the true story of how Jay Payleitner and Rita Page met and fell in love. If mushy romantic tales put you to sleep or turn your stomach, skip to the next chapter, because this is going to take a few paragraphs.

It's fall of my senior year at overcrowded Saint Charles High School. I spent the second half of my lunch hour in the library, where an entire class of juniors was assigned a study hall. Including a cute little brunette with a wicked sense of humor named Rita. I was dating an attractive young lady from the next town over, so I wasn't really looking for love, but still I couldn't help that my natural charm seemed to be winning her over. Or so I thought. It turns out that one of Rita's girlfriends had a crush on yours truly, and Rita had the assignment of filling in that girl on my interests and activities. Later, Rita would tell me her first impression was that I was a little full of myself. Looking back, I probably was.

As the story unfolds, I spent much of my library time memorizing lines for a musical in which I had been cast at the local Catholic girls' school. They needed boys to play the male roles, and I knew several girls from that school, having played in the guitar mass with them at our local parish. I auditioned and was cast as the male lead, Henry Higgins, in *My Fair Lady*.

I hope you're following all this, because this is where it gets amusing. My cute little acquaintance from the library helped me memorize page after page of dialogue for the production. Weeks later, when Rita took her seat in the auditorium, she was a little surprised to see me in the chorus and someone else playing Higgins. She thought, *What a loser—pretending to have the lead role!*

What she didn't know was that the six lead roles in the show had been double cast, allowing for more student involvement. I had performed as Henry Higgins the first two nights but didn't have a single line of dialogue for the final two performances. Fortunately, a closer inspection of the printed program straightened up the confusion.

One other note from the library. My wife has the cutest little opposite of a turned up nose. The very tip actually turns down a bit. Two of our kids inherited Rita's nose, and it's adorable. Well, there in the library I pointed out that she "had a nose like a tapir." Fortunately for me, she didn't know what that was. Unfortunately, we were in a library with a giant 40-pound dictionary. We looked up "tapir" and read the definition. "Any of a genus of herbivorous chiefly nocturnal perissodactyl mammals... that have a heavy sparsely hairy body and the snout and upper lip prolonged into a short flexible proboscis." Adjacent to the definition was a non-flattering drawing of the creature.

That particular encounter didn't go so well, but I will never forget it. As we leaned over the metal stand holding the giant dictionary, I placed my right hand on her lower back. It was a nice moment.

That was fall of 1974. I finally asked her out four months later. Our first date was April 11, 1975, and our third date was my senior prom. I rented a white tuxedo. Rita wore a modest, flowing, green dress with a subdued pattern. As she was walking down the stairs on prom night, her stepdad said, "You can't wear that dress—there are naked ladies on it." Much to all of our surprise, he was right. You had to look close, but the fabric featured several faint images of fairies in various states of undress. Rita's mom saw the humor and overruled her husband, and we had a great time.

I still carry a photo of that young couple in the white tuxedo and naughty green dress. It was in my wallet, and now it's on my phone. More than a hundred times, I've pulled out that photo and passed it around as we told our story to family and friends. When conversations turned to the topic of high school sweethearts, prom memories, or wardrobe malfunctions, that photo became a wonderful storytelling prop.

So what's your story? How did you meet? Our kids have all heard the story of the high school library, the dictionary, the Henry Higgins mix-up, and the naked-lady dress dozens of times. They roll their eyes, but they appreciate the history.

Telling your story is a gift to each other. It may not be as silly as Jay and Rita's. It may be dramatic or romantic. It may also need a bit of careful editing. But I encourage you to tell your story often—it's guaranteed to make you feel closer. Shared history does that. Whenever possible, tell it together. Tag team between his version and her version.

So grab the nearest audience. Kids. Neighbors. Friends. Take a night with your couples' group and have each couple share how they met.

Let me even expand this challenge. Write your story out, include all the juicy bits, and send it to me. Track me down at jaypayleitner.com. If I get enough good tales of love at first sight, meet cutes, and virtuous courtships, I'll present the idea to my publisher. We could call the book, *How We Met*.

— Question to Ask Out Loud —

When was the last time we told our story? Do the kids know it? When did you know that I was the one?

"Jesus spoke all these things to the crowd in parables; he did not say anything to them without using a parable."

—Matthew 13:34

38

Couples Need…

To Know the Traditional Roles

Speaking in front of an auditorium of husbands and wives, I would be a fool to insist that couples should embrace the classic stereotype of the husband as the exclusive breadwinner and the wife as the exclusive homemaker. Frankly, I would risk ostracizing 96 percent of my audience.

Research by NBCUniversal reveals that currently, only 4 percent of families fall under the US Census definition of "traditional": "A working father and stay-at-home mother with kids under 18."[15]

Still, I look back on the way Rita and I raised our kids, and somehow we were fortunate enough to survive mostly on my income—which wasn't always steady and wasn't always enough. Rita did pick up some extra cash by babysitting, crafting, and doing a little bookkeeping for small businesses. For a short period, she even did an overnight bakery job and predawn run as a phlebotomist to nursing homes when things got desperate. But the pressure was on me, and I often felt it.

Over the years, sacrifices were made. Cheaper vacations. More modest Christmases. Non-designer clothing. Less caviar, more mac and cheese. Squeezing in a few more years out of the old clunkers. We were raising five kids on limited and uncertain resources. Does that sound terrible? Even as I type this, the thought overwhelms me: *I miss those days.* We were tight—both our family and our budget.

We didn't necessarily plan it that way. More than 30 years ago, Rita had been recruited by a local realtor to get into the business. At the time, I encouraged the idea because we certainly needed the money and I thought it was something she wanted. As she was about to drop little Alec off at a day care provider for the first time ever, she realized she couldn't do it. I'll quote my wife directly: "No one can take better care of my baby than me. How could they? No one loves that baby more than me."

Of course, every situation is different. And a new generation of moms and dads are turning the traditional roles upside down. The Bureau of Labor Statistics reports that among "dual-career couples, wives earned more than their husbands 28.9% of the time." And according to the US Census Bureau, "Fathers are the primary caregivers for about a quarter of the nation's 11.2 million preschoolers whose mothers work."[16]

More-involved dads? I'm all for that. Husbands and wives talking it out, getting wise counsel, and praying together about what's best for their family during a season of life? I'm all for that too.

I'm also all about the creative kid care options that are springing up with young families. Mom or Dad working part-time from home. Grandma, Aunt Sue, or a dear friend or neighbor loving on your little one a couple days per week. Day care in the workplace.

I mention these options because you may be delaying having kids because you don't think you can afford it. My position—and I've taken some flak for it—is for dedicated parents to have kids early and have a lot of 'em. Smart, hardworking men and women like you, committed to raising confident, productive kids, are generating solutions for the future. Your kids will never be a burden on anyone. They will be a blessing to you and provide answers, leadership, and love the next generation will so desperately need.

In other words, if you wait until you're 100 percent ready, you'll be waiting a long time. And I think you're smart enough to come up with kid care solutions that work for your family.

Back to the question about traditional roles. You don't have to follow them, but you would do well to acknowledge them. And talk about them. They are the elephant in the room.

The same NBCUniversal study suggested that the pendulum of

women flocking to the workforce last century has swung back to women actually expressing a desire for more traditional values. Make note of these two interesting stats:

- Sixty-six percent of moms say they would rather be stay-at-home parents than working parents.

- Fifty-three percent of employed moms feel that while financially they need to work, they would prefer to be stay-at-home moms.

These women are saying that they have a God-given desire to "do the mom thing." Most women who have given birth or adopted a baby have experienced some version of this. Even when women love their careers, almost every new mommy has a hard time severing her maternal ties to go back to work for eight to ten hours every day. Sometimes the depth of feeling and maternal connection surprises them. Waiting for the baby, they fully expected to take a two-month leave of absence and then ease back into the old routine. But after holding their baby, they just couldn't do it.

If you have that feeling, don't brush it away. It's healthy. It's natural. And again, it's something that husbands and wives need to acknowledge, talk about, and turn over to God.

No one—especially this author—is suggesting that the best way for you to connect as a couple is for the woman to stay home, wear pearls and an apron, and have her husband's pipe and slippers ready when he comes through the door.

That is, unless the two of you come to that unlikely conclusion together.

— Question to Ask Out Loud —

When should we have kids? Should we have more kids?

"Behold, children are a gift of the LORD,
The fruit of the womb is a reward.
Like arrows in the hand of a warrior,
So are the children of one's youth.
How blessed is the man whose quiver is full of them."

—Psalm 127:3-5 nasb

39

Couples Need...

To Make Sure the Puke Gets Cleaned Up

All the jobs around the house need to get done. But the division of duties is different for every couple. Let's see how that works in the Payleitner home.

Jay shovels snow, answers the phone, picks up dog poop, scrubs bathrooms, cleans gutters, takes out the trash, trims tree branches, replenishes the salt in the water softener, does taxes, mows the lawn, once a year blacktops the driveway and paints the porch, and yes, cleans up all puke.

Rita pays bills, does laundry, fills the dishwasher, plans weekday dinners, tracks homework, trims hedges, de-glitches computers, shuffles insurance and doctor stuff, remembers birthdays, paints cabinets, feeds the dog, feeds the fish, waters plants, and rearranges the furniture every two months.

For us, what he does and she does is pretty clear. We both have confidence these things will get done even if sometimes it's not the person in charge actually doing it.

For instance, I may tell a capable son or daughter to take out the trash or buy salt for the water softener. One summer I hired a lawn service. One year we took our tax forms to a local accountant. About half the time I hire a crew to seal the driveway, and half the time I do it myself. Rita makes sure dinner arrangements are made, but sometimes that means putting me in charge.

Not all household tasks have a designated doer. First person up gets the newspapers from the driveway and makes the coffee. Last person up makes the bed. Whoever is not busy at the moment picks up the middle school athlete after practice. When company is coming, Jay vacuums. Otherwise, it's Rita's job. We wash windows, attend school events, and rake leaves together.

How were all these assignments assigned? They weren't! Looking back, responsibilities just seemed to fall into place. It came down to passions, giftedness, availability, priorities, and some unspoken factors. For instance, I don't mind scrubbing around toilets. I like shoveling snow. Rita can ignore the sound of an unanswered phone—I cannot. When Rita attempts to clean up puke, there's a high likelihood of more puking. Only I can lift the 40-pound bags of salt, although I'm thinking about changing to 25-pound bags. A few dishes in the sink have never bothered me, but they drive my bride crazy. Rita knows all that confusing medical jargon. If I was in charge of feeding the dog and fish and watering the plants, they would all be dead.

So what's the point? This chapter is a salute to the partnership of marriage. Everything has to get done. And somehow it does. Much of the productivity plan for the Payleitner home evolved without a ton of communication. It just happened. And there's actually very little complaining. Sometimes I hate mowing the lawn; sometimes it's a delightful break in the day. Does Rita like emailing and talking to insurance companies? Heavens no. But she's a master at maneuvering through the maze of claims adjusters and their managers.

I hope your household runs like a well-oiled machine. If not, you might try reassigning some of your daily, weekly, and annual tasks. The division of duties doesn't have to be set in stone. Two decades ago, I tried my hand at paying the bills, but I made some miscalculations that we're still paying for. Rita reminds me that she mowed the lawn for several years—even though we had four growing boys at the time. Go figure. I even loaded the dishwasher once. Rita had to rearrange several plates, glasses, and utensils because I "did it wrong." And—full disclosure—some days the bed doesn't get made!

I continue to be amazed at how very few tasks fall through the cracks. Over the years, the only total failure I can think of is our inability to refill ice trays. Thank goodness for automatic ice makers. Also, dusting has never been a Payleitner priority. Better furnace filters have helped in that regard.

Wrapping up this chapter, a few things to consider. First, don't compare our list to your list. In many families, she does the stinky cleaning details and he deals with computer crashes. Some things—especially any heavy lifting—may seem more like guy stuff. But really, this is all gender neutral.

An informal poll suggests that bill paying duties is split about 50/50 among husbands and wives. Side note: Regardless of who writes the checks or does the online bill paying, both of you should know *where* the money goes.

Also, don't even begin to compare his list with her list. That's a no-win. The factors are too diverse and numerous to consider. Job stress. Season of the year. Season of life. Emergencies. Family dynamics. Cash flow. The best strategy is to just keep pitching in until it all gets done. And keep the lines of communication open. Giving plenty of grace.

Show appreciation for your spouse's hard work:

"Jay, my dear, the lawn looks great."

"Rita, my little IT expert, you saved me again."

Be quick to apologize when something doesn't get done:

"Rita, I'm sorry! The gutters are backed up. I should have cleaned them before the first ice storm."

"Jay, I forgot your brother's birthday. Sorry. Why don't you give him a call."

Give each other permission to point out something that needs to be done:

"Jay, my love, the glasses are spotty. Are we out of salt?"

"Rita, my love, I'm out of clean socks."

Finally, it just isn't a good idea to sit down, put your feet up, sip lemonade, and flip through Facebook or Instagram while your spouse is wrestling with one of those terribly burdensome obligations. If you can help, help! If you can't help, then busy yourself with some minor task or at least go far, far away to relax.

Most importantly—no matter who's in charge—make sure the puke gets cleaned up ASAP.

— Question to Ask Out Loud —

What job(s) have you been doing for a long time that you wish I would do?

"As a dog returns to its vomit, so fools repeat their folly."

—Proverbs 26:11

40

Couples Need...

To Give Their Bedspread a Good Shake

Did you have sex before you were married? Either with each other or someone else?

Sorry if that's blunt. But it's a factor that quite a few brides and grooms bring into their marriage. There's an expression among marriage therapists that the marriage bed is a crowded place. All the old flames are there. Plus your parents. (Yikes.) As well as a flood of ideas you've gathered about sex over the years from movies, books, magazines, and conversations you probably shouldn't have had.

The Bible says, "Marriage should be honored by all, and the marriage bed kept pure" (Hebrews 13:4). And that's just about the best marriage advice you'll find in this book or anywhere. But we're living in a culture that won't help you with that goal. There's a good chance you and your spouse need to initiate a little exterminating so that it's just the two of you remaining between the sheets.

The next page or two may stir up some unpleasant or regrettable memories. You may even discover you need to talk through some issues with a professional counselor. You could ask your pastor or doctor for recommendations. But it's more likely that simply acknowledging that you and your spouse bring different experiences and perspectives into the bedroom will help result in a bit more awareness, patience, freedom, and satisfaction in your own marriage bed.

Past sexual partners can haunt a marriage. Comparisons will be made. There's no need to bring up names or confess past sins or indiscretions with your spouse. That can be terribly hurtful and open wounds difficult to heal. But you have to do more than just shove those memories aside. This is where followers of Christ have a distinct advantage. We have the ability to start fresh—"If we confess our sins, he is faithful and just and will forgive us our sins and purify us from all unrighteousness" (1 John 1:9). An extended prayer of confession— one broken soul crying out to God—is a powerful resource that doesn't get used nearly as often as it should. He's waiting anytime you want to give it a try.

If your husband or wife reveals the need to go to God for renewal, you'll want to support that effort without insisting on details. Your quiet courage to forgive and let it go is critical for anyone who hopes to make a fresh start.

By the way, this process might be something you both need to do. A little patience may also come in handy. But the sooner you arrive at a place of repentance, the sooner you can start to rebuild something bigger, more beautiful, and more satisfying with each other. That's the best way to escape the ghosts of past relationships.

Whether they knew it or not, your parents also influenced your attitudes toward sex. One way or another, they modeled romance in marriage. Growing up, no kid wants to think about their parents doing more than holding hands. But if your parents kissed in the kitchen, count yourself blessed. And what about that awkward sex talk they stumbled through? You should probably give them credit for trying. Did they portray sex as a disgusting, dirty act? Did they express the other extreme with their actions or suggest that anything goes anytime? As long as they settled someplace in the middle, there's a good chance you can work through this successfully.

Indecent movies, romance novels, and pornography also need to be swept out of your bedroom. While you should expect a great sex life, you simply can't model it on someone else's fantasy or images that aren't even real. One of the great joys of marriage is the creative exploration of the needs and pleasures of your beloved. Even after years of marriage, there can be new discoveries and pleasures. Why set your sights on someone else's idea of passion when you can create your own?

The most difficult memories to share from your marriage bed, of course, are sexual abuse or graphic images from your youth. If you're open to healing, it's surprising how effectively and efficiently a good counselor can help you put the past in the past. If you've been scarred by abuse, let your spouse know. Again, you don't have to go over the details. Talking it out with a pastor or professional counselor may be a godsend to your marriage and your life.

This short chapter can only touch on the alarming and serious topic that continues to damage and destroy marriages across our land. Sin, adultery, misdirected lust, abuse, betrayal. You need to know those things are not God's design for marriage. Trust that on the other side of that dark chasm is joy and maybe even a taste of paradise. You really can start building that bridge today.

Do your bedcovers needs a good shake? Have a conversation. Pray together. Whisper your private names for each other. Celebrate your romantic escapades. Laugh about how much you've already learned about each other since your honeymoon. Try something new. Trust each other. Start fresh.

— Question to Ask Out Loud —

Can we start fresh on our own? Or should we find someone else to talk to?

"Come near to God, and God will come near to you.
You sinners, clean sin out of your lives. You who are
trying to follow God and the world at the same
time, make your thinking pure."

—JAMES 4:8 NCV

41

Couples Need…

To Find a Church Home

The first time you heard it, your eyes were opened to a wonderful truth. I've repeated the statement myself scores of times. And I hope you agree: "The church is not a building."

The Bible is quite clear that *people* are the church. First Peter 2:5 describes God's chosen people as "living stones." Ephesians 2:22 explains how we are "being built together to become a dwelling in which God lives by his Spirit." First Corinthians 3:16 confirms, "Don't you know that you yourselves are God's temple and that God's Spirit dwells in your midst?"

Even the Greek word for "church," *ekklesia*, is more literally translated as "called-out ones." Not a building, but living, breathing people.

Got it? The church is not a building.

Still, even though I *am* the church, I still like *going* to church. I like having a permanent, physical location that helps me focus on life outside my own little world. I like when an usher hands me a paper bulletin that includes opportunities to serve or be served. I like shaking hands with a pastor, and I feel good about covering part of his salary. I like looking down the pew and seeing a dozen Bibles open to the same page with people studying the same passage.

At church, I look around and see quite a few people I know and love, and I think, *I feel safe here… We are all in this together… If I were facing a difficult life challenge, just about anyone here would drop what they were doing to help me out.* That's a pretty good feeling.

Most of all, I like what that church building means to my marriage and family. Yes, that's right, the building itself serves as an anchor point. My tithes helped build it. Down the children's hallway, my kids heard biblical truths. In the gymnasium, they raced around Awana circles. In the parking lot and grassy side yard, we met and made friends at annual picnics.

Over our years attending the same nondenominational church at the edge of town, I recall dozens of life-affirming conversations in offices, doorways, and corners of the sanctuary. Those conversations often included prayer, laughter, shared struggles, joyful announcements, and personal invitations to life-changing events I otherwise might have missed.

A church building is a designated place where babies are dedicated, new believers are baptized, dads walk daughters down the aisle, and loved ones are eulogized.

The word "sanctuary" characterizes the entire building. A place of refuge. A safe harbor. A peaceful retreat.

For married couples—after a week that included some squabbles—the short stroll from parking lot to vestibule on Sunday morning might be the first time you've held hands for several days. It's difficult to hold on to anger or petty bickering when the two of you are shoulder to shoulder, sincerely worshipping a God who embodies love, forgiveness, and sacrifice.

So if one of your goals is to connect as a couple, church is a good place to nurture that connection. If nothing else, it's a venue where you can be together once or twice a week and listen to some thought-provoking truths about God and our relationship with him and the world. Talk about those ideas on the way home or over Sunday brunch. If older kids join in the conversation, even better.

One last thought for guys. This Sunday, 13 million more women than men will attend a church service.[17] That seems wrong. Gentlemen, if you are contributing to that lopsided statistic, you're missing out. As spiritual leader in your home, one of your primary jobs is to find a place—yes, a church building—you and your family can call your own.

— Question to Ask Out Loud —

Are we on cruise control when it comes to church? Should we invest more of ourselves? And where do we start?

"The church is not a gallery for the better exhibition of eminent Christians, but a school for the education of imperfect ones."

—HENRY WARD BEECHER

42

Couples Need…

To Sometimes Be
Skipper and Gilligan

Rita and I have agreed to never hang wallpaper together. We tried it once. And then again. And then a third time. But it never ended well. The rooms turned out fine, but we may have had one too many confrontations in the process.

But after hearing the advice of Lawrence and Glenyce Jensen, we might try it again. They explained how one of the secrets to their 67-year marriage was never being comanagers of any potentially frustrating household project.

> A much better plan—modeled for us in the Garden of Eden—is to assign one partner authority and responsibility while the other serves as a helper. Now, the helper is free to offer suggestions and advice, but the leader is the one who decides which course of action to take. The helper must agree to abide by the leader's decisions. In this way, the work can progress, with both partners laboring together in harmony. And if something goes wrong, it's the leader's responsibility—with input from the helper, but no reprehensions—to determine how to make it right.
>
> The next time a task presents itself, pull out a captain's hat (real or imaginary), draw straws, cast lots, or find some other way to figure out who should wear it this time, and hand the other person a first-mate's cap. Or simply say to your spouse, "Okay, today I'm Gilligan and you're the Skipper!"[18]

The reference to the Garden of Eden goes back to Genesis 2:18—"The LORD God said, 'It is not good for the man to be alone. I will make a helper suitable for him.'" Some might argue that passage indicates that the man of the house is always to be in charge of all things at all times, but that idea is probably a little shortsighted. For example, if she's an IT systems administrator and he's a novelist, she clearly should be Skipper for any project that involves setting up a home computer workstation. And if he can't distinguish between moss green, fern, celadon, and olive drab, then he also needs to be Gilligan for the redecorating project.

So you'll probably want to take individual strengths and weaknesses into account when assigning the lead role. But if neither of you has any real expertise, then the Jensens' plan just might work. Choose the project manager by luck of the draw, taking turns, or seeing who has the least busy schedule.

Beyond household projects, identifying a lead decision maker also makes sense in other circumstances of daily life. Surrendering control and unquestioningly accepting all your spouse's choices will keep bickering to a minimum and give the Skipper freedom to try something new. If one of you takes charge of vacation planning this summer, the spouse can enjoy the ride, focus on performing any assignments, and maybe look forward to a surprise or two. If one spouse accepts the role of choosing a restaurant, you can totally avoid the dreaded, "I don't care where we go, where do you want to go?" The Jensens never mentioned the idea of using their system in the bedroom, so we won't either.

In the end, husbands and wives will probably split much of the decision-making and project-leadership assignments of life. When it comes to spiritual leadership and biblical submission, we covered that sometimes controversial issue back in chapter 22.

Finally, to any younger couples confused by the reference to Skipper and Gilligan, clearly you need to watch more bad television sitcoms of the 1960s. To any male readers who grew up watching reruns of *Gilligan's Island*, you may now share with your wife whether you thought Mary Anne was more attractive than Ginger. And why.

— Question to Ask Out Loud —

What household project are we delaying and dreading because we know it will lead to squabbles and hurt feelings?

"I have learned that only two things are necessary to keep one's wife happy. First, let her think she's having her own way. And second, let her have it."

—LYNDON B. JOHNSON

43

Couples Need...

To Talk It Out

I f you and your spouse have never had a conversation end with a door slam or aggressive phone hang up, you can skip this chapter. Everyone else should keep reading.

Disagreements are fine. You *should* bring your own opinions, desires, goals, and life strategies into your marriage. And sometimes his won't match hers. But when conflict arises, you need to keep talking and keep listening until you both see each other's perspective.

Sometimes that takes a while. Sometimes things are said with conviction that need to be taken back. During a conversation—even a heated one—sometimes new information is revealed or a point of confusion is clarified. That can take a while.

Need an example? Let's say a husband states with absolute certainty that going to his wife's family cottage is not an option this weekend. He has an entire list of good reasons—some obvious, some selfish, some practical, and some with which she might not even agree but are important to him. In his mind the case is closed, and he makes a firm definitive statement. "We are not going." But then she gives him some new information. Cousin Kyra was just diagnosed with non-Hodgkin's lymphoma and has expressed a desire to see some of the family members. The husband in our story doesn't know anything about the seriousness or survival rate of that diagnosis. He also doesn't know who else might be at the cottage and all kinds of other information.

Now, this husband genuinely enjoys spending time with cousin Kyra, and besides, he is the nicest, most compassionate guy in the world. But remember, he has already made a clear definitive statement based on a considerable amount of information. That's not always easy to take back. There are issues like trust, loyalty, and personal pride involved. When a man (or woman) of integrity takes a stand, it's a good thing to not be wishy-washy and change your mind every two seconds.

In a marriage, when either spouse makes a definitive, clear-cut, unambiguous statement, it should be honored almost universally. If brash, uninformed declarations are made seven times a day without consulting your spouse, that's another issue. But in general, firm decisions are good things. They are the first step to getting things done in life. "We'll take this house." "I'm joining the army." "We're leaving for church at 9:40." "I'm ordering a pizza."

All that to say, it might require a few minutes for the husband to consider this new information, weigh all the facts, and retract his definitive statement. If this guy's bride has slammed the door, run away in tears, or aggressively disconnected the call, then he hasn't been given the time to do that 180-degree turn he needs to make. It takes more than three seconds to turn the *Titanic* around.

There's an oft-quoted verse that seems to say a husband and wife should never go to bed angry. "'In your anger do not sin': Do not let the sun go down while you are still angry, and do not give the devil a foothold" (Ephesians 4:26-27). But there's much more to that verse than kissing and making up before going to sleep.

First, that portion of Scripture suggests that it's acceptable to be angry sometimes. But it also comes with a warning. We need to handle our anger properly. We can't let it boil inside us. We can't let it push away people we care about. And if new information becomes available, we have to give all parties involved a reasonable amount of time to reconsider and recalibrate.

Don't allow the conversation to end until the two of you are on the same page again. That's hard. There may be long periods of silence. More than one declarative statement may have to be taken back. Apologies may need to be spoken, heard, and accepted. Sometimes you have to leave for work, take a time-out to get additional information, or dial down the exchange because the kids enter the room.

Sometimes the sun does go down and the discussion needs to be tabled until later. But no matter what, don't give Satan that foothold.

So talk it out. Give it time. Work toward being on the same side again. Try desperately not to say anything you'll regret later. But if you do, it's always best to apologize early, honestly, and with a truly repentant spirit.

Finally, put it behind you. On the drive to the cottage, it does no good to rehash the debate or belittle his dozen original reasons to not make this trip. As a matter of fact, any spouse who courageously changes their stance should be given bonus points, extra credit, and heaps of appreciation for being the kind of bighearted person who listens, considers all the options, and has the courage to change their mind. That's not the easiest thing to do.

— Question to Ask Out Loud —

Which one of us is more likely to storm out of a room or slam down a phone when a conversation should actually keep going?

"Consistently wise decisions can only be made by those whose wisdom is constantly challenged."

—Theodore Sorenson

44

Couples Need...

To Conspire for a Higher Purpose

D o you like compliments? Do you like hearing people saying, "You guys are awesome," "I'm so glad you made this happen," or "I can never thank you enough"?

Wouldn't that be nice to hear? Wouldn't that make you feel as if you've accomplished something together? Praise like that is just about a sure thing if the two of you were to launch a neighborhood Bible study.

The kudos and compliments will be authentic. If you held a regular outreach for the people who live up and down your street, in your apartment building, or in nearby farms, the lives of real people might be radically transformed. Your entire community could be swept with a fresh spirit of love and friendship. Scores of individuals may even come to know Christ as their Savior. That's all nice, of course. But I can't emphasize enough that boldly inviting people into your home to talk about Jesus will make your own marriage stronger, your love deeper, and your kisses sweeter.

Are you with me? Or are you thinking, *Jay, that sounds impossible...maybe I'll just move on to the next chapter?*

Well, it's not as difficult as you think. There are resources to guide the way. There are people living right nearby who would eagerly say yes to such an invitation. And the Bible encourages the idea of purposefully gathering in small groups.

> Let us think of ways to motivate one another to acts of love and good works. And let us not neglect our meeting together, as some people do, but encourage one another,

especially now that the day of his return is drawing near
(Hebrews 10:24-25 nlt).

Who would come? And why would they bother? Well, some may
simply be curious about meeting the neighbors or seeing your deco-
rating. But the truth is, you don't know what kind of struggles and
conversations are going on in kitchens and bedrooms within steps of
your own home. People are hurting and looking for answers. Many
are lonely, bored, and in need of friendship. Some have moved to your
neighborhood with spiritual gifts that are being wasted. All of us are
looking for purpose.

Even though such an outreach would be a big deal, don't make it
sound like one. Send out 20 invitations—by email, mail, phone calls,
or knocking on doors—that say, "We're starting a monthly gathering
to talk about where God is in the world today. Just for a few neighbors. Come for coffee and dessert…" Schedule it for 90 minutes on
an upcoming slow weeknight. You'll very likely get positive responses
from about one-third of those invited. And then take it from there.
Meet once a month or more often. Open your Bibles together to a
familiar chapter in Luke or John. Make it engaging, helpful, and fun.
That's right, fun.

A few things you need to definitely *do*:

- Do stand around the kitchen for the first 15 minutes,
  introducing people and chatting about kids, sports,
  weather, and so on. Then move to a sitting room.

- Do have a very basic Bible study prepared.

- Do have extra copies of the Bible in a readable translation.

- Do ask questions of the group, not singling out individuals.

- Do end on time.

- Do serve three different awesome desserts.

- Do be available if anyone wants to stay longer or talk about
  a personal challenge.

And things in the *don't* category:

- Don't preach. Don't be churchy. Don't invite your pastor.

- Don't ask people to read aloud.

- Don't put anyone on the spot.

- Don't be scholarly or give easy answers to tough questions.

- Don't talk about church, religion, politics, or controversial issues.

Finally, do rely on the Holy Spirit. If you attempt this kind of event under your own power, it may not go so well. Also, don't think you need to provide all the answers to every question that may come up. Keep it simple. In the New Testament, Paul reminds the church in Corinth that his initial sermons were not about using fancy words or being in the spotlight. He was a brilliant scholar and orator, but when Paul first entered their lives, he spoke simply about Jesus.

> When I first came to you, dear brothers and sisters, I didn't use lofty words and impressive wisdom to tell you God's secret plan. For I decided that while I was with you I would forget everything except Jesus Christ, the one who was crucified. I came to you in weakness—timid and trembling. And my message and my preaching were very plain. Rather than using clever and persuasive speeches, I relied only on the power of the Holy Spirit. I did this so you would trust not in human wisdom but in the power of God (1 Corinthians 2:1-5 NLT).

You may be surprised to find this kind of suggestion in a book on how to connect as a couple. Indeed, if hosting a neighborhood Bible study is way, way out of your comfort zone, please put it on the way, way back burner. But the direct benefits of this kind of partnership for husbands and wives still apply. Having a shared ministry and implementing a project that honors God will bond your marriage more than a carriage ride in the park or a weekend at a bed-and-breakfast.

Maybe the turnout will be disappointing. Maybe no one will have experienced a life-changing Damascus Road experience. Maybe the crust on the strawberry rhubarb pie was a little burned. Still, when you close the door after the last guest leaves, I promise you'll look at each other and say, "That was worth the effort."

— Question to Ask Out Loud —

If we were to partner together on a ministry project, what might that be? With whom could we partner? And whom might we serve?

"It is easier to love humanity than to love your neighbor."

—Eric Hoffer

45

Couples Need…

To Be Tourists in Their Hometown

Imagine some dear friends from out of town coming to visit your hometown for exactly one week. They've got a reasonable budget and have assigned you with the task of keeping them busy seven days straight with two sightseeing adventures and two dining experiences per day.

The goal is to find 14 destinations and 14 dining experiences within a short driving distance. What's on that list? In 20 minutes of brainstorming, the two of you can come up with an itinerary filling much of the week. Invest another hour on the Internet, and you can finish the list with destinations off the beaten path and maybe even get specific information about special events that weren't on your radar. If you still need more ideas, visit your local chamber of commerce or tourist center.

Here are categories of things you might consider. Out-of-the-way restaurants. Local delicacies. Authentic mom-and-pop pizza joints. Brunches and buffets. Sidewalk cafés. Bakeries, chocolatiers, and ice creameries. Historic landmarks. Galleries. Factory tours. Trollies, cruises, and double-decker buses. Stadiums and arenas. Public gardens. Sculpture parks. Botanical gardens. Nature hikes. Haunted houses. Concert venues. Planetariums. Sports tournaments. Butterfly conservatories. Picnic spots. Beaches. Amusement parks. Walking tours. Outlet malls. Shopping plazas. Tourist traps. Observation decks. Aquariums and zoos.

Don't forget seasonal activities specific to your region. Like cherry blossom festivals, clam digging, apple picking, strawberry picking, Mardi Gras, harvest celebrations, local festivals, county fairs, state fairs, and annual hot-air balloon launches.

Got your list? Print it off and post it on your fridge. Of course, this exercise is not about out-of-town friends. It's about the two of you. And it's not a plan for a single week. It's a plan for the next 14 weeks. Each week, you and your beloved should plan on crossing off one dining experience and one activity on this customized list. Three months from now, you'll have more memories than you can imagine. All without leaving home.

Often we think the best way to connect as a couple is to take a $5000 luxury cruise, drive six hours to a bed-and-breakfast in another state, or fly across the country for a week of hotels and upscale restaurants. Not so. As a matter of fact, if you expect your marriage to sparkle based on a once-a-year extravagant fling, you'll put way too much pressure on yourself that week.

Come to think of it, if you choose to do the 14/14 project, you'll want to hold that loose as well. If you miss a week or skip an event, it's all good.

One benefit might be that you find a new restaurant or destination to which you can return time and time again. A comfortable place you can bring out-of-town friends and family members for years to come. A place that's an extension of home.

— Question to Ask Out Loud —

Where have we never gone that we always wanted to—within 20 minutes of home?

"There is nothing like staying at home for real comfort."

—Jane Austen

46

Couples Need…

To Reach Back

I'm on record admitting that men need to apologize more often than women. That's because we mess up more. We're risk takers, we sometimes act before considering the consequences of our actions, and we speak before thinking about the repercussions of our words. This shortcoming of ours should not come as a surprise to women.

What wives may not know is this. When a husband messes up, nine times out of ten he knows it instantly. He knows he tracked mud on the kitchen floor. He knows he left the milk on the counter overnight. He knows he should have checked the date with his wife before ordering those playoff tickets. You really don't have to pile on.

He also has a reasonable explanation for each of his minor failures. He had to come inside to get better cell reception on an urgent phone call. He cleared everything else on the counter but got distracted because the dog needed to go out. The tickets were almost sold out.

Now, it may appear as if he's oblivious to his transgressions. That's because he's waiting to see how the sequence of events plays out before deciding what his next step should be. He's also trying to determine whether the teeny-tiny damage will disappear on its own.

In the meantime, his loving bride points out the crime, which means a confrontation is a definite possibility. Because he knows he messed up, he's going to apologize. Since it was a minor infraction, it shouldn't be a big deal. "Hey sweetheart, forgive me for the mud prints." "Sorry, babe. So you *don't* like sour milk?" "That's my bad. I totally should have checked with you first."

This next moment is the turning point for this particular issue. With his low-key apology, he is essentially reaching out. She has two choices—maybe three. She can reach back and let it go. Or escalate the attack.

Ladies, I urge you to reach back simply and gently. "No problem." "Not a big deal." "We'll figure it out." That response works because he already knows what he did and the lesson has been learned. Case closed.

On the other hand, a wife certainly may choose not to accept the short and sweet apology. But she needs to know that if she chooses this option, the attention is no longer on her husband's *actions*. She will have chosen to attack his *character*. Does she really want to do that?

If his intent was evil or if there is a larger flaw that needs to be addressed, then maybe she should take a stand and make her case. What looks like a minor infraction could very well be a critical flaw or part of a destructive pattern that shouldn't be brushed away.

In a marriage, if one of you does something truly hurtful, then any apology needs to go way deeper than simply reaching out. There needs to be a sincere acknowledgment of the damage. Plus some kind of willingness to turn over a new leaf and make amends. Then it's really up to the offended spouse to extend a significant measure of grace. Maybe the two of you need to set aside time together to get to the root of the transgression and even ask our heavenly Father for clarity and guidance. All of which may take some time, days even.

Anytime wives and husbands disappoint each other, the goal is reconciliation. If it's a reoccurring character flaw or deliberate cruelty, then I encourage you to pursue some help beyond anything found in this chapter or even this book. An apology is a good start, but it's only the first step toward repentance, repair, and restoration.

But if your relationship can be fully restored with a sincere reach out and a simple reach back, that's a sweet deal you shouldn't pass up.

Allow me to make one more suggestion for wives. If your husband's biggest wrongdoing is something minor—tracking mud, leaving milk out, bad calendar math—you may want to count your blessings and put a positive spin on the entire episode. You should still expect an apology. But add a "punishment" that fits the crime. Wrap your arms around his neck—hugging, not choking—and with a devious smile say something like: "Mud on my kitchen floor? That will cost you an hour of window washing or a hike in the woods with me. Your choice." "On your way home from getting a fresh gallon of milk, you're going to have to stop at DQ and grab me a Cookie Dough Blizzard." "Hey, Buddy. Whatever you spent on those playoff tickets, you're going to have to spend on me when the season is over."

I'm well aware this chapter sounds like I'm bashing husbands. Really, it's just that I'm so experienced at apologizing that the chapter just leaned that way. It should go without saying that it works both ways. Men, when your wife messes up and reaches out, you need to reach back as well.

So let's all become masters at the quick apology. It's so much nicer to put things in the past then to drag them out over and over again. When those silly little quibbles are allowed to linger, they lose their silliness and really start to stink.

— Question to Ask Out Loud —

Is there any silly little thing hanging over our marriage right now that needs a quick apology? How about any not-so-silly *big* thing?

"The end of argument or discussion should be, not victory, but enlightenment."

—JOSEPH JOUBERT

47

Couples Need...

To Build Hedges

I am not about to accuse any reader of adultery. Or accuse anyone of even thinking about adultery.

But we're human. And we make mistakes. And there are times in every marriage where the husband or wife are just inches from a slippery slope leading to disaster and they don't even know it.

Correction. They *do* know that they've stepped outside the safety zone, but they think they can handle it. That's a red alert.

Let's consider two totally fictitious scenarios in which guys and gals might tempt fate.

An athletic guy joins a coed rec league—softball, soccer, volleyball. His wife is home with the little ones and even encourages her wonderful hubby to go burn off some steam two nights a week. It's all good. This guy is just trying to stay in shape and have some fun. A sweet, outgoing, young single gal happens to be on the team and appreciates his athleticism. There's natural team camaraderie and friendly high fives after every nice play. If you add a little sweat, some adrenaline, and an impromptu victory celebration at a local tavern, there's a high likelihood that those two teammates will flirt a little. It may go no further than that, but it might.

A marketing manager comes back from maternity leave and isn't feeling real attractive. Her husband was supportive through the pregnancy, but sleepless nights and lack of intimacy are taking their toll. Her husband has not said "You look great" for about a year. But the guy from sales has said those exact words a dozen times in the last month.

He's not really flirting. He just appreciates her style and smile. Seeing the guy from sales is about the only time during the week when she *does* smile. Before long she starts texting him for sales projections she doesn't even need. Throw in some late dinner meetings or a business trip, and we've got a formula for a marriage on the rocks.

Both the athletic guy and the marketing manager in our stories were faintly aware that they had crossed a line. It wasn't when he joined the league or she met with the sales guy. The problem had nothing to do with making new friends or doing good work. But at a moment in time they crossed into the danger zone.

Has that ever happened to either of you? Did you ever find yourself giving a little too much attention to a member of the opposite sex? Signs to look for include simply thinking about that other person during the course of your day. Finding a reason to spend more time with that person. Subtly tracking that person's whereabouts so you can run into them "accidentally." Giving them a gift—even a silly little trinket. Asking to share a cab or car ride to an event. Having his or her photo on your phone. Deleting texts they send. People mistaking you for a couple. Avoiding the mention of that other person's name to your spouse. Talking about that person with your spouse as a way to deny your growing attachment. And, of course, feeling the Holy Spirit convicting your heart but ignoring the battle waging within.

One huge danger sign is when you start noticing lots of little faults in your spouse. (If you look, you'll find some. We all have them.)

If you're in the danger zone, the first thing you need to do is admit it. In his book *Hedges: Loving Your Marriage Enough to Protect It,* bestselling author Jerry Jenkins pulls no punches:

> Quit kidding yourself. Understand the tremendous capacity of every human being to deceive himself or herself when not connected to God. Know that, once you start making excuses for wrong behavior, each excuse will sound more plausible, and you will sink deeper and deeper into sin and ruin. Admit that you can't trust your own self apart from God, and decide to stay close to Him.[19]

Second, don't blame the sports gal or the sales guy. Don't blame any individual who may smile at you, flirt a little, or speak words you wish your spouse would say. This is on you. It's *your* marriage that needs protection. It's time to step back from the situation very quickly. In other words, "Flee from sexual immorality" (1 Corinthians 6:18).

Third, build some hedges. Choose ahead of time to avoid situations that lead to temptation. Even steer clear of situations that have the *appearance* of temptation. Take dramatic steps as needed. Literally find a way to spend less time with that person. Quit the team. Change accounts. Start going to a different gym or book club. If you can't avoid that person, then be cold toward them. Other hedges include talking more about how wonderful your spouse is and doing the stuff in the other 51 chapters of this book.

Finally, don't try to avoid sexual temptation under your own power. Any hedge you plant by yourself won't be high enough or prickly enough. Pray. Ask God for direction. Confess any lust, lies, or covetousness to God. "Watch and pray so that you will not fall into temptation. The spirit is willing, but the flesh is weak" (Matthew 26:41). Make sense?

Sorry if this chapter seems like a downer. But you can't possibly connect as a couple if there's an unspoken third party strolling through the imagination of you or your beloved.

Build that hedge. And hey, what were you thinking, anyway?

— Question to Ask Out Loud —

What hedges have we put in place? Do we need to add any hedges? Where?

"If the grass looks greener on the other side of the fence, it's because they take better care of it."

—Cecil Selig

48

Couples Need...

To Not Believe Everything They Hear About Marriage

As you've noticed, I appreciate a well-constructed quotation. Especially when the writer takes an indisputable truth and phrases it in a manner that's fresh, revealing, and perhaps even life changing. A few examples come to mind:

> *"One advantage of marriage is that, when you fall out of love with him or he falls out of love with you, it keeps you together until you fall in again."*
>
> —JUDITH VIORST

> *"The family you come from isn't as important as the family you're going to have."*
>
> —RING LARDNER

> *"Love seems the swiftest, but it is the slowest of all growths. No man or woman really knows what perfect love is until they have been married a quarter of a century."*
>
> —MARK TWAIN

Those are quotes I used to punctuate three chapters in my book for men, *52 Things Wives Need from Their Husbands*. Now, you can see those quotes are really just saying, "Stick with your marriage," "Don't use the past as an excuse for the future," and "Love grows over time."

But the writers have given them a structure and flow that lend them a bit more credibility and weight.

Funny thing about quotations. You can't trust 'em. For every believable wise saying, there's another one that says the exact opposite:

"Too many cooks spoil the broth."	*"Many hands make light work."*
"Look before you leap."	*"He who hesitates is lost."*
"Opposites attract."	*"Birds of a feather flock together."*
"Don't judge a book by its cover."	*"Clothes make the man."*
"Better safe than sorry."	*"Nothing ventured, nothing gained."*
"Absence makes the heart grow fonder."	*"Out of sight, out of mind."*

Which is it? In each case, perhaps both hold a grain of truth. But they can't both be 100 percent right. Those looking for answers may be led down the wrong path.

Following is a list of deep, thoughtful insights on marriage...that are just plain wrong. At least that's this author's opinion. See if you don't agree.

"Marriage is a lottery in which men stake their liberty and women their happiness."

—Madame Virginie de Rieux

"Love-matches are made by people who are content, for a month of honey, to condemn themselves to a life of vinegar."

—Marguerite Gardiner, Countess of Blessington

"It destroys one's nerves to be amiable every day to the same human being."

—Benjamin Disraeli

"The secret of a happy marriage remains a secret."

—HENNY YOUNGMAN

"Marriage may be compared to a cage:
the birds outside frantic to get in and those inside frantic
to get out."

—MICHEL DE MONTAIGNE

"Happiness in marriage is entirely a matter of chance."

—JANE AUSTEN

"To marry a woman who you love and who loves you
is to lay a wager with her as to who will stop loving the
other first."

—ALBERT CAMUS

"Marriage has no natural relation to love.
Marriage belongs to society; it is a social contract."

—SAMUEL TAYLOR COLERIDGE

"Marriage is like a dull meal with the dessert at the beginning."

—HENRI DE TOULOUSE-LAUTREC

"Marriage must incessantly contend
with a monster that devours everything: familiarity."

—HONORÉ DE BALZAC

"But let there be spaces in your togetherness,
And let the winds of the heavens dance between you.
Love one another but make not a bond of love."

—KAHLIL GIBRAN

Is marriage really a cage, a lottery, a social contract, a secret, a life of vinegar, a dull meal? I think not. It's only a cage if you feel trapped. Marriage is not some game of chance or a social contract—it's God's plan. If a marriage contains secrets, uncovering them is part of the great joys of life. And the pursuit of new ways to express love is hardly vinegar or a dull meal.

Finally, does anyone still quote Kahlil Gibran or have a faded poster hanging in their den with that gibberish to leave "spaces in your togetherness" and "make not a bond of love"? It's utter nonsense. Creating a bond of togetherness and love is the goal of every married couple I know.

So don't believe everything you read or hear about marriage. Consider it carefully through the lens of God's Word. And talk it over with your beloved. You'll find that marriage leads to gifts discovered, happiness doubled, grief divided, simple joys appreciated, and lifelong contentment shared.

— Question to Ask Out Loud —

What's your favorite benefit of marriage? And should we get it made into a poster?

"The man who finds a wife finds a treasure,
and he receives favor from the LORD."

—PROVERBS 18:22 NLT

49

Couples Need…

To Take a Fresh Look at the Love Chapter

When newlyweds today open their wedding gifts, do they still get overdosed with 1 Corinthians 13:4-8? Back in October 1979, Rita and I found some of those verses on half of the cards we opened. Plus two plaques, one framed print, and a poster. I remember thinking, *Oh, that's nice.* But not, *This is life changing.*

But you know what? It *is* life changing. And the "love chapter" of the Bible can be marriage saving. You've seen it before. But this time, make a little extra effort to actually consider what it says.

> Love is patient, love is kind. It does not envy, it does not boast, it is not proud. It does not dishonor others, it is not self-seeking, it is not easily angered, it keeps no record of wrongs. Love does not delight in evil but rejoices with the truth. It always protects, always trusts, always hopes, always perseveres. Love never fails (1 Corinthians 13:4-8).

Okay, now read it again. But don't read it as a definition of love. Also, don't read it as a list of activities you need to check off. *Hmmm, let's see. 1. Be patient. 2. Be kind. 3. Be content…"* Instead, read those five verses as a promise.

Sometime down the road, that promise is going to come in handy. Or maybe it's a promise you need to grab on to today.

Are you afraid of falling out of love? Worried that the spark of young love has dimmed? Maybe you've heard too many divorced couples—perhaps even your parents—say, "We just fell out of love." When couples say those words to friends, or when parents say those words to their children, it sounds like a convenient excuse. But those couples who have severed their marriage vows really believe that the overwhelming love that once brought them together is gone. It just went away. The loss can't be explained. One day they loved each other, and then one day they did not.

That's pretty scary, isn't it? And that fear is justified if people all around you seem to be choosing divorce.

What should you do? Instead of being afraid, do just the opposite. Expect it. Anticipate it. Plan for it. Know that sometime, you're going to look at your husband or wife and think, *Where's the love? Who is this person I'm married to? What's missing?*

As terrifying as that sounds, you need to trust the promise of love. Trust that in the very near future, the entire emotional tidal wave of feelings we equate with love will once again wash over both you and that person with whom you exchanged sacred vows. And the fear will be gone.

Until next time.

When the feeling comes that you are "falling out of love," the absolute worst thing you can do is panic. When you panic, you do things you regret later. You say things that hurt and, unfortunately, continue hurting your spouse even after the gushy love feelings come back. Your imagination takes an unfortunate turn, nurturing a fantasy life outside of your marriage commitment. Online, you search names of old flames. Instead of just smiling at the new human resource assistant, you start to flirt—just a little. Men find excuses to work late or start clicking on porn sites. For women, romance novels gain a new appeal, and you start bashing your husband to your girlfriends.

Instead of turning your imagination loose, consider how much you have to lose. As lonely and distant as you feel, your spouse feels exactly the same. Please don't put up a barrier between yourself and the one person who also is afraid, who also wants to feel love again.

While panic brings trouble and regret, the promises of 1 Corinthians 13 bring hope. Trust the power of love to do what it does best. Love has an inherent staying power. As long as you and your bride have not given up, love will not fail. It might not *feel* like it, but love is still there. You may feel as if you're drifting further apart or traversing a desolate wasteland, but when you come out on the other side, love will be stronger, deeper, and more passionate than ever.

So instead of panicking, consider going back to the basics. Spend time together. Do what friends do. Do what lovers do. Talk it out. Remember the past. Envision the future. You didn't always love each other, but you grew into love.

Your wedding vows were really a public commitment to trust love. In any given season—especially during the years when careers are being built, kids are requiring constant attention, and exhaustion rules the day—it may be difficult to even remember that feeling of first love. Be patient. There will come a time when you once again see your spouse across a crowded room and your heart will say, "There's my love."

— Question to Ask Out Loud —

In what ways have we grown since our wedding day?

"I didn't marry you because you were perfect. I didn't even marry you because I loved you. I married you because you gave me a promise. That promise made up for your faults. And the promise I gave you made up for mine. Two imperfect people got married and it was the promise that made the marriage…And when our children were growing up, it wasn't a house that protected them; and it wasn't our love that protected them—it was that promise."

—THORNTON WILDER, *THE SKIN OF OUR TEETH*

50

Couples Need…

To Rebuild Love

If something's missing from your marriage, maybe it's time to go back to the drawing board. To consider what forces forged love in the first place. To go back to the basics. Back to boy meets girl.

Let's examine the stages that took you from first impression to marriage proposal and see which part of the relational assembly line has broken down. As any production manager will tell you, the factory output is only as efficient as its weakest link.

Attraction may be the first building block of love. What was it that attracted you to each other in the first place? Was it physical, relational, emotional? A smile. A kind word. An air of independence, playfulness, or style. A twinkle in the eye. Or was it a sense of presence or confidence you felt when they walked in the room? Who was initially drawn to whom? Or was it mutual? It might have been sudden. It might have been gradual. Spend a moment. Delight in that memory. Meditate on that first awareness of your attraction to each other until it comes back. It's still there. Or it can be if you want it to be.

Moving on. The second building block of love is *communication*. It may have been easy; it may have been awkward. Somehow the two of you started to make beautiful music together. There was a verbal chemistry, including both small talk and real talk. Why did you care about what the other was saying? At some point, you let down your guard and dared to talk about hopes and dreams. Frustration and fears. More than once you talked all night. That's when you knew. Can you still talk like that? Go ahead. Talk like that.

In the act of constructing love, what comes after looking and listening? *Respect.* Somehow you began to do more than talk, flirt, and laugh. You began to see all sides of each other. Fun/serious. Intense/easygoing. Spiritual/searching. Experienced/incomplete. Smart/gullible. All grown up/just a kid. Your future spouse became for you a puzzle, and unscrambling the secrets within became a high priority. Do you still see the complete, complex man or woman with whom you fell in love? Or maybe you only see one side. Regardless of how long you've been married, you still need to encourage each other to explore your many sides and many gifts. That's respect.

Love can't begin, however, until you reveal your own needs and begin filling each other's needs. It's been said men don't like to reveal their vulnerabilities. And women are just the opposite. The truth is, we all need to be needed, and that's why you began to fill in each other's gaps. In other words, *provision.* As a couple, he begins where she ends. What he can't do, she can. Let's admit that in many ways, men are still the hunters, the cabin builders, the fire starters. Women are the nurturers, healers, nourishers. As seasons turn and relationships evolve, roles will change. Marriage works best when both provide for both.

Closely tied with provision is *protection.* Men and women also share the responsibility of protecting each other—and loved ones—from threats both physical and emotional. Standing watch. Locking doors. Keeping wolves and grizzlies at bay. Maintaining order. Enforcing rules. Staying focused on the big picture. Attending to details. Rising up with incredible latent power when your home and ideals are under attack.

Finally, when we find a man or woman worthy of all of the above, we have one more step to take, one more decision to make. *Exclusivity.* That's when we can bring our laser-like focus onto the goal of uniting with one soul mate for the rest of our lives.

Wiser men than me have attempted to define love. But these six elements come pretty close to describing how love should act. Attraction, communication, respect, provision, protection, exclusivity.

Husbands and wives, are you falling short in any of these areas? Consider each element one at a time as it applies to your own commitment and contribution. If there's work to be done, take personal responsibility for strengthening that particular foundational piece of your relationship.

See if your entire marriage isn't stronger because of your intentional, sacrificial commitment to love.[20]

— Question to Ask Out Loud —

Are you still committed to being attractive, communicating, respecting each other, providing for and protecting each other, and exclusively giving your heart to the one you married?

---

*"Love at first sight is easy to understand;
it's when people have been looking at each other for a
lifetime that it becomes a miracle."*

—SAM LEVENSON

51

Couples Need...

To Feel Safe

Would you consider it a risk to come back from running errands one afternoon with a tray of professional watercolors, two or three camel hair paintbrushes, and a pad of 100 percent cotton watercolor paper?

If it's something you've been thinking about—dreaming about—for more than a year, why *wouldn't* you stop by Hobby Lobby this Saturday? You could pick up everything you need plus a sturdy beginner's easel for less than a hundred bucks. You've already thought about where you would set it up. You already know the kind of subjects you'd be painting. A few weeks from now, you might even have something worth framing and hanging on your wall forever. It wouldn't be a masterpiece, but it would be a start.

What's the worst that happens? You throw away eighty bucks? You spill some paint on the carpet? You come to realize painting isn't as easy as it looks? That's actually a good thing. Rising to meet a challenge is a healthy part of developing yourself as an artist. Discovering you're absolutely terrible might not be pleasant, but at least you'd know, and you could begin to dream about something else. None of these things are the end of the world.

Actually, the worst thing that could happen would be that your spouse laughs at you. And maybe even mocks you for trying. Does that fear keep you from trying new things?

A wife belittles her husband's dream to build a sailboat. A husband makes a snide comment because she tells people she's writing a novel, but she's been stuck on the third chapter for more than a year. Crushing words from a thoughtless spouse come easily, don't they?

"If you run for school board, you'll have to talk in front of people, and you're terrible at public speaking."

"You can't replace the hinge on the bathroom cabinet, but you think you're going to build a coffee table?"

"The worship director said she wants people who can actually sing."

"Piano lessons? Not sure I want to listen to 'Twinkle, Twinkle Little Star' for the next year."

"A blog? What would you write about that someone else would want to read?"

If you dared to share a personal dream with your spouse, would you hear words like these? If you hinted you might like to do something a little challenging or go someplace a little out of the way, is that person you love and trust going to douse your dream with a bucket of ice water?

Well, fear no more. You need to feel safe and even encouraged to try new things. Whether those are hobbies you've been mulling over for years or some things you just want to try on a whim.

Bookmark this page. Find the right moment. And ask your spouse to read this chapter. Let them know you *need* their support.

There's a good chance they don't even know they're doing it. They might be trying to protect you from failure. They might be scared that you're learning and growing while they're stagnating and standing still. Maybe they're jealous. Maybe they are sniping back at you because you haven't been supportive of their dreams. Or maybe they think they're being funny.

Spouses need to feel safe to stretch themselves and try new ventures. More than that, spouses need to empower each other to chase their dreams. If you can pursue those dreams together, that's even better. But when one of you wants to try something new—on your own—the other needs to lead the cheers. Maybe even try phrases like these:

"Go for it."

"That's impressive."

"Anything I can do to help?"

"Beekeeping? Wow. I don't know anything about bees, but I do like honey."

"That's an excellent use of the spare bedroom."

"For sure, that's something we can fit in the budget."

"Just when I thought I had you all figured out, you surprise me with this hidden talent. You continue to amaze me."

"I will be your biggest fan."

One reminder to all you wives and husbands who are surprised when your spouse takes up a hobby seemingly out of the blue. There's a good chance they've been thinking about it for a while. So choose your comments carefully.

On the other hand, if you are guilty of wasting upward of five hundred bucks starting a new hobby every year or so, don't be surprised if the reaction you get is less than enthusiastic.

In any case, the goal is for either of you to take half the credit when your spouse sells their first million-dollar painting. After all, you were the inspiration, right?

— Question to Ask Out Loud —

What is one hobby, career goal, or dream you've considered but never talked with me about? I promise I'll listen.

"Make it your goal to create a marriage that feels like the safest place on earth."

—GARY SMALLEY

52

Couples Need...

To End Their Days Well

In this chapter you are going to meet George and Winerva from Seattle and Tim and Debbie from Wheaton. I'm jealous of how they spend the last few minutes of their evenings.

Every night, George and Winerva open their Bible and read a chapter aloud. Over their 56 years together, it's been foundational to their marriage. A rare business trip, an illness, or some other distraction may have caused them to miss a night. It's not an obsession—it's a sincere desire to get closer to God, which assuredly means they will get closer to each other.

The nightly rhythm they've settled on is straightforward. They typically read a single chapter and spend a moment or two sharing an insight. They move the bookmark to the next chapter and kiss good night. That doesn't sound hard, does it?

George and Winerva estimate they've read through their King James Bible eight or nine times. If some new insight strikes one of them, they may stop and park on a particular verse for a while, which means they don't get through an entire chapter. Once in a while, they'll read more than one chapter. At breakfast and supper, they often did short devotionals with their four girls. But the nightly time with Scripture was a husband and wife thing.

You can imagine what that commitment has meant to their marriage and family. Just think about the verses they came across. In Leviticus, they read and talked about the meaning and application of the words, "Ye shall be holy: for I the LORD your God am holy" (19:2 KJV).

In Ruth, they read, "Whither thou goest, I will go; and where thou lodgest, I will lodge: thy people shall be my people, and thy God my God" (1:16 KJV).

In Ezekiel, they read, "I will take away the stony heart out of your flesh, and I will give you an heart of flesh" (36:26 KJV).

In Revelation, they read, "Blessed is he that readeth, and they that hear the words of this prophecy" (1:3 KJV). George and Winerva's resolve inspires me.

My friends Tim and Debbie trace their own nightly routine to a challenge Tim heard at a men's retreat early in their marriage. An older man dared the men to pray out loud daily with their wives. Tim and Debbie have been faithful to that strategy for more than 25 years. Their nightly investment of time is not long or laborious, and it even ends with a song.

Tim's and Debbie's prayers usually focus on the kids, extended family, missionaries they support, or other needs expressed by members of their church family. They also pray for each other, which seems to be a powerful way to end each day. Tim even gave me permission to reveal the last thing they do. The "Amen" to their prayer triggers a silly love song they sing to each other. It's to the tune of "We Love You, Conrad" from the 1960s musical *Bye Bye Birdie* and includes some original lyrics Tim was not eager to share with the world. He said, "Only our kids and a handful of very close friends have been blessed by it. On camping trips, where we were all together in one trailer, our kids looked forward to hearing it every night."

From Seattle to Chicago to every state and every country, I'm quite sure millions of couples pray together each night—or each morning—right out loud. That consistent time of wives and husbands coming before the Lord doesn't make the nightly newscast. These faithful men and women rarely talk about it, nor would they boast about some kind of special blessing they deserve. Their prayers don't instantly negate all the dark forces overtaking the world. But that time together most certainly has a supernatural impact on their marriages. Covering them with a protective shield and securing God's favor in a way the rest of the world won't believe or understand.

Thanks to George, Winerva, Tim, and Debbie for giving us, perhaps, the number one way a husband and wife can connect as a couple.

— Question to Ask Out Loud —

Should we commit to praying for 90 seconds together in the morning or at bedtime? Which Bible should we use to read out loud to each other?

"Unless the LORD builds the house, the builders labor in vain."

—PSALM 127:1

Notes

1. "Divorce begets divorce—but not genetically," Indiana University news release, July 11, 2007, http://newsinfo.iu.edu/news-archive/5982.html.

2. Sara McLanahan and Gary Sandefur, *Growing Up with a Single Parent: What Hurts, What Helps* (Cambridge, MA: Harvard University Press, 1994).

3. Deborah A. Dawson, "Family Structure and Children's Health and Well-being: Data from the National Health Interview Survey on Child Health," *Journal of Marriage and the Family* 53 (1991): pp. 573–84.

4. Peter Hill, "Recent Advances in Selected Aspects of Adolescent Development," *Journal of Child Psychology and Psychiatry* 34 (January 1993): pp. 69–99.

5. Wade Horn and Andrew Bush, "Fathers, Marriage, and Welfare Reform," Hudson Institute Executive Briefing (Indianapolis, IN: Hudson Institute, 1997).

6. Adapted from Jay Payleitner, *52 Things Wives Need from Their Husbands* (Eugene: Harvest House, 2012), pp. 93–95.

7. Adapted from Jay Payleitner, *52 Things Husbands Need from Their Wives* (Eugene: Harvest House, 2013), pp. 91–94.

8. Leigh Lumford, "There Are 338 Drive-In Theaters Left in America—Here's Where to Find Them," *Nerve*, http://www.nerve.com/entertainment/drivein-theater-open-find-location.

9. Adapted from Payleitner, *52 Things Husbands Need from Their Wives*, pp. 121–23.

10. "Not the Turn-Off You'd Expect, Doing Household Chores Actually Turns Up the Romance," *PR Newswire*, February 11, 2013, http://www.prnewswire.com/news-releases/not-the-turn-off-youd-expect-doing-household-chores-actually-turns-up-the-romance-190661171.html.

11. The four statements ending this paragraph are from Peggy McDonough, Vivienne Walters, and Lisa Strohschein, "Chronic Stress and the Social Patterning of Women's Health in Canada," *Social Science and Medicine* 54 (2002), pp. 767–82; Scott J. South and Kyle D. Crowder, "Escaping Distressed Neighborhoods: Individual, Community, and Metropolitan Influences," *American Journal of Sociology* 102, no. 4 (January1997), pp. 1040–84; Allan V. Horwitz, Helene R. White, and Sandra Howell-White, "Becoming Married and Mental Health: A Longitudinal Study of a Cohort of Young Adults," *Journal of Marriage and Family* 58 (November 1996), pp. 895–907; and Stephanie A. Bond Huie, Robert A. Hummer, and Richard G. Rogers, "Individual and Contextual Risks of Death Among Race and Ethnic Groups in the United States," *Journal of Health and Social Behavior* 43 (2002), pp. 359–81. All cited in the Heritage Foundation, "The Benefits of Marriage," *FamilyFacts.org*, http://www.familyfacts.org/briefs/1/the-benefits-of-marriage.

12. Corey L. M. Keyes, "Social Civility in the United States," *Sociological Inquiry* 72, no. 3 (2002), pp. 393–408. Cited in the Heritage Foundation, "The Benefits of Marriage," *FamilyFacts.org*, http://www.familyfacts.org/briefs/1/the-benefits-of-marriage.

13. John MacArthur, "The Rape of Solomon's Song, Part 2," *Grace to You*, https://www.gty.org/resources/Print/Articles/A397.

14. Adapted from Payleitner, *52 Things Husbands Need from Their Wives*, pp. 65–67.

15. NBCUniversal, "Moms Aspire to Be Modern Day June Cleavers, According to a New Women at NBCU Study Which Paints a Dramatically Altered Picture of Today's American Family," *PRNewswire*, October 4, 2011, http://www.prnewswire.com/news-releases/moms-aspire-to-be-modern-day-june-cleavers-according-to-a-new-women-at-nbcu-study-which-paints-a-dramatically-altered-picture-of-todays-american-family-131020118.html.

16. Bureau of Labor Statistics, "Table 25: Wives Who Earn More Than Their Husbands, 1987-2009," *Women in the Labor Force: A Databook: 2011*, http://www.bls.gov/cps/wlf-table25-2011.pdf.

17. "This statistic comes from Barna's figures on male/female worship attendance, overlayed upon the Census 2000 numbers for adult men and women in the U.S. population." Church for Men, "Quick Facts," http://churchformen.com/men-and-church/where-are-the-men/#sthash.XjV3h Nrx.dpuf.

18. Robin Schmitt, *Married for Life* (Hallmark Gift Books, 2004), pp. 50–51.

19. Whitney Hopler, "Plant Protective Hedges Around Your Marriage," *Crosswalk.com*, September 8, 2005. Adapted from Jerry Jenkins, *Hedges: Loving Your Marriage Enough to Protect It* (Wheaton: Crossway Books, 2005).

20. Adapted from Payleitner, *52 Things Wives Need from Their Husbands*, pp. 77–78.

More Great Harvest House Books
by Jay Payleitner

52 Things Husbands Need from Their Wives

Jay digs deep to give practical, doable, fun, and unexpected ideas for a wife to connect with her husband by listening, remembering he's a man, encouraging him with her words, making space for him to participate, respecting him, and appreciating his "hero moments." Great steps for strengthening a marriage!

52 Things Wives Need from Their Husbands

For the husband who wants to live out God's plan for his marriage, *52 Things Wives Need from Their Husbands* provides a full year's worth of advice that will put you on the right track without making you feel guilty or criticizing you for acting like a man. A great gift or men's group resource.

What If God Wrote Your Bucket List?

Most bucket lists seem to be filled with fluff that has zero eternal value. Surely God has a better plan. Jay suggests 52 unexpected items for your bucket list to usher in purpose and joy today...and leave a legacy that just might make God smile.

52 Things to Pray for Your Kids

How do you raise your kids up into godly young adults? Jay knows the power of sustained prayer over his children. With practical insight into praying for your children's health, safety, and character, this resource will help you pray powerfully for children of any age.

52 Things Kids Need from a Dad

Straightforward features with step-up-to-the-mark challenges make this an empowering confidence builder with focused, doable ideas; uncomplicated ways to be an example; tough, frank advice, like "throw away your porn"; and *no* long lists or criticism for acting like a man. Great gift or men's group resource!

52 Things Sons Need from Their Dads

These 52 quick-to-read chapters offer a bucketful of man-friendly ideas on building a father-son relationship. By your life and example, you can show your boy how to work hard and have fun, often at the same time; live with honesty and self-respect; and develop the inner confidence to live purposefully.

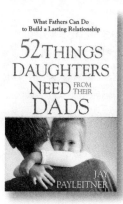

52 Things Daughters Need from Their Dads

Jay guides you into "girl land," offering ways to do things *with* your daughter, not just *for* her; lecture less and listen more; be alert for "hero moments"; and give your daughter a positive view of the male sex. You'll gain confidence in building lifelong positives into your girl.

365 Ways to Say "I Love You" to Your Kids

You adore your kids, but expressions of love can get lost in the mayhem of daily living. Jay inspires you to show your affection, pride, and joy with 365 simple ideas that will encourage and nurture your child one loving moment at a time.

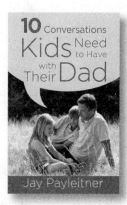

10 Conversations Kids Need to Have with Their Dad

Straightforward, man-friendly advice about communicating all-important life values to your kids. Plant healthy thoughts about *excellence, emotions, integrity, marriage, immortality,* and five other key character qualities. A terrific, confidence-boosting resource for building lifelong positives into your family. *Great gift or men's group selection.*

It's Great Being a Dad

Jay joins veteran dads Brock Griffin and Carey Casey to offer their best practical advice so you can build awesome relationships with your kids. In partnership with the National Center for Fathering, they draw on their day-in, day-out experience to help you engage with daughters and sons in the very best ways.

The Dad Book

Jay has packed this handy volume full of quick, inspiring help:

- fresh suggestions for engaging your kids
- dad-to-dad humor
- ways to *show* your kids instead of *tell* them
- encouragement and ideas to help your kids connect with God

Great confidence-booster for dads of any age and stage!

The Dad Manifesto

This pocket-size collection of tips, tricks, and tidbits provides the inspiration you need to become the best dad you can be. Each page features a fun project, a creative experience, or an important commitment that will help you establish a connection with your kids that will last a lifetime.

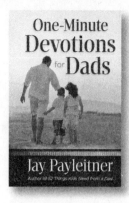

One-Minute Devotions for Dads

Jay knows how regular guys think because he is one. His 125-plus coaching sessions—devotions, if you must—offer unexpected but relevant topics and touches of wacky humor. They'll encourage you with seasoned wisdom and God-centered thinking. *Great gift.*

About the Author...

Jay Payleitner is a popular speaker on marriage and parenting, and the author of more than 15 books, including the bestselling *52 Things Kids Need from a Dad*, *The Dad Book*, *52 Things Husbands Need from Their Wives*, and *What If God Wrote Your Bucket List?* One of the top freelance Christian radio producers in the United States, Jay has worked on *Josh McDowell Radio*, *Today's Father*, *Jesus Freaks Radio* for the Voice of the Martyrs, *Project Angel Tree* with Chuck Colson, and many others. He is also creator of "The Dad Manifesto" poster and book. Jay has served as an AWANA director, a wrestling coach, and the executive director of the Illinois Fatherhood Initiative. He is also an affiliate of the National Center for Fathering. Jay and his wife, Rita, live near Chicago, where they've raised five great kids and loved on ten foster babies. Best of all, Jay and Rita have four grandkids...and counting.

To learn more about Harvest House books and
to read sample chapters, visit our website:

www.harvesthousepublishers.com

HARVEST HOUSE PUBLISHERS
EUGENE, OREGON